The Blocked Writer's Book of the Dead

Bring Your Writing Back to Life!

David Rasch, Ph.D.

The Blocked Writer's Book of the Dead
Bring Your Writing Back to Life!
David Rasch, Ph.D.

Copyright 2010 David Rasch, Ph.D.

All rights reserved. No part of this book may be reproduced or transmitted, in any form or by any means now known or to be invented, electronic or mechanical, including photocopying, recording, or by any information storage or retrieval system, without written permission from the author, except for inclusion of brief quotation in a review.

Illustration page 4 © The New Yorker Collection 2004. David Sipress from cartoonbank.com. All Rights Reserved.
Cover photo of Isis, Egyption Goddess of Magic and Protector of the Dead, by David Rasch.
Text and cover design by Patricia Hamilton.

Park Place Publications
P.O. Box 829
Pacific Grove, California 93950
www.parkplacepublications.com

Printed in the United States of America
First Edition January 2011

For my mother, Adele

Acknowledgments

I would like to express my gratitude to several people who helped with the creation of this book. My editor, Laurie Gibson, provided invaluable assistance with reviewing and editing several versions of the manuscript. The final product has been vastly improved by her suggestions and exquisite attention to detail. Patricia Hamilton skillfully and cheerfully guided me through the publication process. I am indebted to her for many valuable contributions with formatting, cover design, and a host of other essential aspects of book publishing.

Ken Jones, Harold Grice, Deanne Gwinn, Joyce Krieg, Mike Thomas, Wanda Sue Parrott, and several other members of the Central Coast Writers branch of the California Writer's Club have provided inspiration, contacts, and resources that have assisted me considerably on my writing journey. My Stanford colleagues Fred Luskin, Hilton Obenzinger, Larraine Zappert, and the staff of the Stanford Faculty/Staff Help Center have all offered helpful input and support with my writing at various points through the years.

I am especially grateful for my daughters, Meehan and Alison, who had to hear quite a bit about writer's block throughout their formative years. Their fresh wisdom and good humor has been a delight that quietly boosts my energy to write. Finally, I would like to thank my wife, Ixchel, for her unfailing encouragement, advice and love as I encountered the many joys and challenges involved with writing and publishing a book.

Contents

Dedication		3
Acknowledgements		5
Chapter 1	Why Blocked Writers Need a Book of the Dead	9
Chapter 2	Death is Inevitable; Writing is Not	13
Chapter 3	Know Thyself	17
Chapter 4	Past Lives and Write Now	37
Chapter 5	The Grateful Blocked	41
Chapter 6	Motivations for Writing	47
Chapter 7	A Room, Womb, or Tomb of One's Own	52
Chapter 8	House Training the Writer Within	59
Chapter 9	Procrastination: The Sickness Unto Deadline	69
Chapter 10	Not in Your Write Mind	80
Chapter 11	Feelings	90
Chapter 12	The Judgment	93
Chapter 13	Encountering the Unknown	105
Chapter 14	Rebirth: Improving Writing Productivity	110
Chapter 15	Your Writing Productivity Improvement Plan	115
Appendix	The Puppy Principles	123
Bibliography		124
About the Author		128

CHAPTER 1

Why Blocked Writers Need a Book of the Dead

"… bring me the water-pot and palette from the writing kit of Thoth and the mysteries that are in them."
~ *The Egyptian Book of the Dead*

"I can only write when deadlines have passed and I feel like there is a gun to my head. Even then it takes enormous effort to make myself do it, and I can only write in intense, long binges where I neglect everything else in my life. Afterwards I feel completely drained. I hate writing."

"I have too many other commitments to find time to write. I know my publishing record will be the single most important factor in my tenure review, but somehow I lose sight of that because I feel overwhelmed with the demands of teaching and other administrative tasks. Maybe it's a way of avoiding writing."

"I've been working on the book forever, but I don't seem any closer to the end. I spend hours in the library and I'm always discovering more books I need to read before I can feel confident about what I'm writing. I've rewritten my first chapter so many times I've lost track of why I even began writing this book."

"I have plenty of time to write but I waste enormous amounts of time on insignificant tasks or just sleeping. I dread actually sitting down at my desk and beginning to write. I'll find any excuse to do something else. No one knows how serious a problem this is and I lie when my friends ask how my book is coming along."

"I don't belong here. The university made a huge mistake hiring me as a professor. There's no way I'll ever be able to get published in a respectable journal. If I try to write anything it will be obvious that I am out of my league. I have this terrible recurring fantasy of a group of graduate students reading an article I've written and laughing out loud. Unfortunately, I'm not suited for any other kind of work and I'm terrified of failing."

"Whatever I write seems like absolute crap to me. I can spend hours on a single paragraph, only to tear it up in disgust. What made me think I could be a writer? I'm terrified that I don't have what it takes but I can't give it up. Every day I feel haunted by thoughts of what I am not accomplishing."

Inspiration for writing this book

My inspiration for writing this book came from my experiences over two decades as a therapist, teacher, consultant, and group leader for writers with productivity problems. The previous statements are typical of what I hear from the writers I work with. This book is a guide for people who are seeking to understand and resolve problems with initiating, sustaining, and completing writing projects. The title came to me when I realized that in writing a self-help book, I was contributing to a genre whose origins can be traced to *The Egyptian Book of the Dead,* which was probably mankind's very first self-help book. This remarkable text includes passages written as early as the third millennium B.C. that instruct spirits of the dead on how to achieve immortality and eternal happiness in the afterlife.

Bring Your Writing Back to Life!

Writing was an essential element of burial for the ancient Egyptians, at least for those who could afford it. They had their "books of the dead" carved into the stone walls of their tombs or written on papyrus rolls placed in their sarcophaguses. These writings were believed to be indispensable aids for contending with death and the afterlife. It was thought that only by reading the verses in their tomb or sarcophagus would the disembodied spirits know how to attain immortality and overcome horrific adversaries in the next world (such as fierce crocodiles, enormous snakes, and ass-swallowing demons). These post-mortem challenges sound daunting indeed, but many living writers of books and dissertations confront equal, if not greater, horrors. They need a book of the dead too.

My title was also inspired by another ancient classic of self-help literature, *The Tibetan Book of the Dead*. It was written in the eighth century A.D. and attributed to the teachings of Padmasambhava, a Buddhist saint. *The Tibetan Book of the Dead* is supposed to be read aloud over the bodies of the recently deceased. It describes the perils and opportunities that their souls will encounter in the "bardo," a spiritual dimension encountered after physical death and before the next rebirth. Death and the subsequent trip through the bardo is described as a time of great opportunity for those who have the proper training, guidance, and presence of mind to respond skillfully to the many challenging emotions, distractions, traps, and rewards that characterize that realm.

The Tibetan Book of the Dead

The Tibetans believed that the recently disembodied soul encounters a host of frightening and seductive phenomena in the post-mortem trip through the bardo, which must be properly handled to prevent an automatic rebirth into another confused and painful existence on the earth, or worse. I think of the writing process as a type of bardo, because those of us who write (like spirits leaving the body) enter into a complex and challenging realm of experience and are confronted directly with the remarkable, mysterious, and vexing

Hope, possibility, power, mystery

realities of our lives, habits, hearts, and minds.

In fact, several themes addressed in both the Tibetan and Egyptian books of the dead are relevant to the experience of writing. These include encountering the unknown, understanding the nature of suffering and struggle, cultivating awareness, acting wisely, recognizing and facing danger, working skillfully with difficult emotions, asking for help, learning patience, communicating effectively, and attaining liberation from habits that trap us. Books of the dead are also about hope, possibility, power, mystery, and rebirth into greater worlds. They instruct about the paths toward transformation that appear when all seems lost. These themes are as relevant for living writers as they are for dead ones.

CHAPTER 2

Death is Inevitable; Writing is Not

All we have to do is wait long enough and death will come. Waiting for writing to occur is less of a sure bet. Writing is a mentally demanding and complex activity that requires sustained effort and attention. Numerous neurological processes connected with speech, motor activity, memory, emotion, visual perception, word and sentence construction, and sound recognition light up the brain during the process. We have to mentally and physically coordinate all this activity in order to produce intelligible written documents. It's demanding, and the mechanics of writing are susceptible to breaking down in many ways.

In my work I listen to stories of how people avoid writing. The magnificent energy and creativity of the human mind is seldom so exquisitely manifested as when it is devising methods of defeating the intention to write. If these elaborate schemes of avoidance could be regarded as high art instead of deadly sin, blockers would be a proud and happy lot. We would only go to such extraordinary lengths to avoid writing if there were compelling reasons to do so. Do any of the following ring true for you?

To start with, you have to do it by yourself. It is a solitary undertaking, and you need to be able to tolerate loneliness, self-

Why writing can be tough

doubt, fatigue, dread, delayed gratification, uncertainty, criticism, and overwhelm—yet still continue to write. Others can encourage you in various ways, but at the end of the day, it's you alone who must actually make yourself do it.

Writing is a sum of many diverse mental activities, behaviors, and relationships that somehow combine to create a finished product. These include generating ideas, making notes, organizing those notes, both expanding upon and refining ideas, building phrases and sentences, creating drafts, revising drafts, seeking feedback, final editing, dealing with criticism, praise, or rejection of the final work ... then getting into your next project. You have to perform all of these tasks, and be able to decide when to move back and forth between them. Hundreds of decisions and corrections of those decisions must be made, even with short pieces. Your perseverance, judgment, patience, and confidence are constantly put to the test.

In addition, for better and worse, your ability to write is intimately connected with your psychological state. If you take the time to closely examine what actually goes on in your mind moment to moment, it quickly becomes apparent that you have less control over your thoughts and feelings than you might want to admit. A typical psyche is a seething cauldron, bubbling with impulses, emotions, random ideas, habitual thoughts, creativity, logic, fantasies, sensory perceptions, desires, and conflicts. Your intention to write must assert itself from within this roiling psychic miasma, despite the fact that some of these internal dynamics are not supportive of your writing agenda. It is *your* own mind, supposedly, but it doesn't always mind you.

Writing is also hard because you are always confronting time-consuming biological and social realities like the need to sleep, eat, earn money, and spend time with your family and friends. Because time and energy are limited, choosing to write often requires a sacrifice of some sort in other areas.

Writing becomes even more difficult if important people in your life do not support it. This includes loved ones who feel neglected, colleagues and mentors who are neglectful, competitive, or threatened, as well as parents and lovers who don't understand what you're doing or who consider writing a lousy career choice or a waste of time.

In addition, despite your best intentions, you can easily be derailed from writing by the compelling and ubiquitous Siren songs of hot baths, television, conversation, parties, e-mail, the Internet, phone calls, the cookie jar, and the compulsion to scrub tile grout with a toothbrush.

Being productive is also hard if you have had inadequate or incorrect training. Writing requires that our brains and bodies learn a complex set of neurological and behavioral operations that do not occur naturally. If that training was done poorly or interrupted, writing may be experienced as being especially arduous, distasteful, and time consuming.

Many of the writers I work with recall painful or traumatic experiences connected with writing from their pasts. Upsetting remarks and negative reactions from teachers, parents, or other important figures have a strong impact on young minds and create intense feelings about writing such as resentment, fear, and self-doubt. To make things worse, few of us were taught anything useful in our educational system at any level about how to overcome writing blocks or other common problems with writing productivity. You usually have to figure these things out on your own, and it is difficult to find competent assistance if you even think to seek it.

You also take personal risks when you write. You are producing something for public scrutiny that could expose you to negative judgments and criticism. What if writing is your passionate dream

Taking personal risks

and your writing makes people angry, bored, or disappointed? If you don't write, other people may also get angry and disappointed. If your ability to write productively is essential for career goals such as completing an educational degree, achieving tenure in academia, or making a living as an author, the pressure to produce can be a motivating force, but it can also generate crippling anxiety spirals and work stoppages.

Clearly, the personal challenges associated with being a writer are not trivial. In my experience, to have at least occasional problems of some sort with beginning or sustaining writing is more the norm than the exception, even for writers with experience and success. If writing never seems difficult, you have indeed been blessed (but I would counsel you not to speak extensively about this blessing in the company of other writers).

CHAPTER 3

Know Thyself

The "blocked writer" who stares in anguish at a blank page or who repeatedly rips up work in frustration is a widely recognized cultural archetype that appears frequently in books, cartoons, movies, and conversation. But what is "writer's block"? I became curious about this question in the early days of my work with writers. I was counseling highly motivated, intelligent people seeking help with performing a seemingly straightforward task. I should have been able to help them, yet somehow I was managing to fail spectacularly. Why? I couldn't decide whether my clients were lazy, recalcitrant, and uncooperative or whether I was just a remarkably inadequate therapist. Over time I was able to see that writing productivity problems are quite complex, subtle, and tenacious, and that I had to look more deeply into the nature of these difficulties and facilitate change more skillfully.

Writer's block is not a single, identifiable syndrome. People use the phrase, as I do in this book, to describe a variety of difficulties that result in a halt or significant decrease in writing productivity. As previously mentioned, writing is a complex, multifaceted enterprise and it breaks down in many different and interesting ways. The various forms of writing block often share common themes such as perfectionism, procrastination, overwhelm, anxiety, and fear of criticism, but each person's writing process has

Writer's block is not a single syndrome

its own unique context, history, and specific pattern of behavior, thoughts, and feelings. I recommend starting the journey with a thorough exploration of the problem, and encourage you to seek a very specific understanding of the assets and liabilities of your own writing process. This will help you craft a plan for improving your writing productivity that is well thought out and has a good chance of succeeding.

Writing Productivity Problems

Below is a list of common difficulties reported by blocked writers. It is not an exhaustive list, and the categories should not be viewed as rigidly defined or mutually exclusive. As you read through it, make a note of the items that seem relevant to your writing process.

◉ *Time and Scheduling Difficulties*

Writing by conscious planning or by unconscious default

Many writers with productivity problems have trouble with *time*. You must find time, protect it, and then use it well despite the competing pulls of other responsibilities, people, pleasures, and the complex workings of your mind. Every day, through conscious planning or by unconscious default, you prioritize your activities and make decisions about how to spend time. It can be quite a challenge to determine how much time the writing portion of your life requires, and to incorporate that into a workable routine. It may require some maneuvering to insert regular blocks of writing time in your daily and weekly schedule, and even if you find the time you are still faced with the daunting task of sticking to the schedule and actually writing something during the minutes or hours you've carved out.

Common problems with time and scheduling include:

- *An inability or reluctance to make future plans about writing*
- *An inability or reluctance to schedule your day*
- *An inability or reluctance to stick with a schedule you have made*
- *Losing track of time, getting distracted*
- *Chronic lateness*
- *Overbooking your time*
- *An inability to estimate how long a task will take*
- *Overwhelm and anxiety when thinking of the future*
- *Working too long at a stretch*
- *An inability to write except just before or after deadlines*
- *Insufficient prioritizing of writing relative to other activities and commitments*
- *Over-focusing on the passage of time and worrying that time is too short*

Writers often struggle to manage time

Understanding your issues with managing time will also be a topic on page 27: **Assessing Your Writing Productivity Problems**.

◉ *Difficulty Starting*

I have worked with several writers whose primary challenge was taking the step of sitting down at their desk. Their anticipatory anxiety or other resistances create a mental barrier against taking the first step. Often they are entertaining an inaccurate and exaggerated estimate of the agony that will ensue if they write. I love to swim but I dislike getting into the water due to the brief shock of the initial chilliness. I spend a good bit of time on the deck, contemplating and postponing my entry, but once I dive in and do a couple of laps, I'm plenty warm and I enjoy being immersed. Writers who have difficulty starting often do fine once they have taken the plunge, and the challenge is to learn to set up one's writing life to increase the odds of diving in. This will be discussed in more detail in the subsequent chapters, **A Room, Womb, or Tomb of One's Own** and **House-Training the Writer Within**.

⊙ *Rejecting Ideas Prematurely*

This tendency involves thinking of ideas then rejecting them before they have been considered sufficiently or written down. Generally this idea-rejecting process takes place privately in the solitude of the individual mind. Ideas arise and are not written down because of a feeling that they are not "good enough."

You have to be able to tolerate the raw quality of your first thoughts in order to let them out of the privacy of your cranium and allow them to exist nakedly in black and white. Often they look different on paper than they seemed in your head, and you can evaluate them more objectively. The process of writing down rough ideas in the early stages of a project should not be viewed as a waste of time. Once ideas are written down, even if they embarrass you, they have been preserved and can be reflected upon and improved over time. You are not proclaiming they will be the final product just because you wrote them. It is a step in the process that permits you to develop your thoughts more fully and generate additional ideas and inspirations. The act of actually writing words also stimulates creative thoughts in a way that does not happen when the words exist only in your mind. Freewriting is an exercise that can be very useful for developing the skill of writing without involving your inner critic in the process. It is the practice of writing down whatever

Writing stimulates creativity

occurs to you without pausing or judging the content. Peter Elbow's book, *Writing Without Teachers,* gives a great explanation of how to understand and work with freewriting.

⊙ *Freezing Up or "Drawing a Blank"*

This problem often takes the form of staring blankly at your paper or monitor and being unable to think of what to write next. Typically there is a sense of anxiety that accompanies this behavior, which grows as time passes without any thoughts or words arriving. You might also start getting anxious about the fact that you are anxious, because you know that anxiety interferes with writing. As this anxiety spiral intensifies it becomes even harder to think clearly or produce writing. Anxiety inhibits abstract thinking, interferes with short-term memory, and can wreak havoc on productivity.

⊙ *Procrastinating*

This is one of the most common behaviors associated with writing, and it takes many forms. Briefly defined, procrastination is the avoiding of writing that one wants or needs to do, even though one is capable and interested in doing it. Procrastination frequently occurs in alternation with intense, desperate episodes of rushed writing under deadline pressure. The varieties of thoughts, feelings, and behaviors associated with procrastination are extensive, and though I should describe them now, I think I'll do it later (see Chapter 9, **Procrastination: The Sickness Unto Deadline**).

Working Long Hours with Little to Show for It

Some very energetic and disciplined writers find they are unable to move their projects forward effectively. They don't appear to avoid work and they are willing and able to put in long hours, but somehow meaningful forward progress eludes them. Below are some of the ways this happens.

⊙ *Excessive editing or rewriting of early drafts*

This approach makes the experience of writing slower and more stressful. Significant mental energy is required to solve editing problems while simultaneously trying to generate ideas. Elements of perfectionism are commonly associated with this premature microscopic scrutiny of the fine points of an early draft. Frustration, doubts, fears of failure, distaste for the process, and eventually a disinclination to write are all aspects of this syndrome. Having said this, I must also acknowledge that some very successful writers prefer to write this way and I don't recommend changing approaches that work for you. But if you write this way and it leads to frustration and work avoidance, then you may need to address it.

⊙ *Getting lost or hiding in research*

Often writing projects require that a certain amount of background research be conducted. Some writers have difficulty making the transition from gathering information to producing writing. Research is interesting and it's less demanding than creating sentences and paragraphs that someone else will read and evaluate. Most writers love to read and some are tempted to indulge their enjoyment of reading beyond what the project really requires. Spending excessive time doing research on the Internet, in the lab, or at the library may also arise from the need to reassure yourself that you know absolutely everything about the subject in order to prevent any possibility of experiencing the humiliation that comes from making a public mistake. Writers must do enough research to do their job well, but if you've only been reading and taking notes, and several years pass, this might signal a problem.

⊙ *Commitment difficulties*

These challenges are characterized by numerous rewrites that are not refinements of an initial draft, but are rather repeated excursions into entirely new approaches driven by excessive self-doubting. A certain amount of reconsidering and overhauling should be viewed as a healthy part of the creative process, but when doubt becomes the dominant psychological driver, a descent into agony and frustration may ensue. Usually this pattern is connected with a fear of committing to a particular line of thought, because once that commitment is made you feel vulnerable to criticism or failure. What if your choice is not the "right" or "best" one? What if you have made a crucial but unnoticed mistake that will undermine the whole project? So you rewrite to assuage your anxiety by using a different approach in an unending search for the perfect passage. People caught up in this cycle are often plagued with doubts to the degree that they can no longer recognize, appreciate, or effectively develop their own good ideas. The internal stress generated by this dynamic is considerable.

⊙ *Overworking, difficulty with stopping*

The compulsion to push too long and too hard is marked by the loss of healthy life balance as the writing project becomes an obsession. Overworking is different than having episodes of inspired immersion in work, which are typically experienced as a good thing by writers. People who overwork have become monomaniacal about their involvement with writing to the point that creativity and productivity suffer. Other common consequences are burnout and difficulties in relationships, health, and happiness. As odd as it may sound, for these writers, learning when to *stop* writing each day improves the quality and quantity of output.

⊙ *Including too much peripherally related material*

Learning when to stop writing

You have to be able to decide what is important and what is not to make progress moving a project ahead. There is always more to be said about any subject, and those writers who keep adding peripheral material and lose touch with the main focus of the work are less productive, even if they work long hours. Often they find the editing process to be grueling. Editing decisions are not always easy and writers can lose a lot of time agonizing over what to leave in and what to take out. Some people find it very hard to remove anything from their drafts out of fear that they might be excising something vital. Editing questions are unavoidable and have no perfect answers, but when the default position is to leave everything in "just in case," things can get very bogged down.

Difficulty Finishing

Some writers work well until they reach the end of their project. Then everything stops. Putting the final touches on and presenting it as "finished" arouses uneasy feelings. These writers may have several nearly completed manuscripts. When one project is almost complete they move on and start the next. Apprehensiveness about public exposure and judgments typically drives this pattern. One young faculty member in my class who had written prolifically was denied tenure for his undistinguished publishing record because he was unable to finish any of his several papers and submit them to journals. After the wake-up call of his tenure denial he addressed several projects with renewed vigor and completed them all.

Psychosomatic Barriers

I worked with a graduate student who had neck spasms whenever he attempted to write. The spasms pinched a nerve that caused his writing hand to go limp. Through our discussions it became clear that the muscular contractions in his neck were connected with his rage toward an advisor who was excessively critical and inconsistent. His limp hand possibly symbolized the hopelessness he felt trying to win his advisor's approval. This is an example of a psychosomatic writing problem. The physical experience made the writing difficult or impossible, but recognizing his feelings of rage and powerlessness was necessary to facilitate change. Other common examples of psychosomatic barriers are headaches, fatigue, hand cramps, dizziness, and nausea, when these symptoms are generated by emotional conflicts.

Physical Problems

I have seen many people whose ability to write was limited by health issues. These situations are heart wrenching when the desire to write is strong but the body is weak in some critical way. Repetitive stress injuries from keyboard use are sometimes tragically debilitating, and awareness of correct ergonomics is important for those who write.

I worked with one assistant professor who was denied tenure because her chronic arm and wrist pain made keyboard use excruciating, and she was unable to complete enough work. Her efforts to heal the injuries were begun too late, and alternative technologies such as voice-recognition software were not yet effective enough. If you spend a lot of time writing on a keyboard, it's worth the time to learn how to minimize the likelihood of such injuries through proper posture and positioning of your computer. This is especially true if you are beginning to experience neck, arm, or wrist pain; there is good information available on the Internet regarding what you can do.

Difficulties with Sharing Writing and Dealing with Criticism

There are those who write fluently but are unable to show their work to other people. Being private about one's writing can be simply a matter of preference, as in personal journal writing, but it is a problem for those who desire publication, feedback, editing help, or other assistance. You may have learned that it was unsafe to expose your writing due to traumatic experiences in school or elsewhere. It's helpful to learn how to deal with the inevitable criticism and rejection that comes from showing others your work, without getting too devastated or blocked. Finding the right people to involve with your writing process at various stages is important, and this topic will be explored in Chapter 2, **The Judgment**.

Gender, Race, Culture, and Writing Blocks

Over the history of Western civilization, the production of written texts has been overwhelmingly the province of fair-skinned males. Fortunately this is changing, but numerous personal, professional, and societal hurdles still exist for writers from the less empowered segments of society, and these realities can contribute to writing problems. Confidence crises, hopelessness, and self-doubt may be more difficult to overcome for those who have learned that their efforts will not be noticed or valued.

Securing access to helpful educational opportunities, collegial support, publishers, and professional networks has traditionally been harder for women and individuals from minority groups or foreign cultures. I have also worked with several writers who were not native speakers of English who were blocked due to lack of confidence in their command of the language. Appropriate encouragement and practical support goes a long way toward releasing the potential of individuals with these additional challenges as writers.

Rejection, Criticism, and Interpersonal Issues

Writing may seem like a solitary enterprise, but there are a variety of interpersonal issues that impinge upon writing productivity. Most people are sensitive to the reactions and opinions of others, and writers frequently have their confidence and self-esteem challenged when either anticipating or reacting to encounters involving criticism and rejection. Productivity can be enhanced by steadily improving one's ability to control anxiety and tolerate feedback. It is not uncommon for blocked writers to have too few people to talk with about their writing. Issues of embarrassment, shame, unworthiness, and depression sometimes contribute to an unhealthy isolation.

The act of connecting with other writers can be a powerful way to generate renewed passion, confidence, and energy for writing. Isolated writers, however, frequently find the social, emotional, and psychological barriers to reaching out to be formidable, and recommendations for change must be carefully considered.

The impact of personal relationships on the writer is another complex area in which productivity-related issues may arise. Our personal relationships may include people who have strong opinions about our writing life. They may assist or interfere with our productivity in subtle or overt ways. To a certain extent this is an unavoidable reality and learning to keep both personal relationships and a writing life going is a challenge for many writers.

Connecting with other writers

Mental Health and Neurological Issues

Depression and anxiety are frequent visitors to those who struggle with writing. Sometimes depression and anxiety arise primarily because the writing is not happening. I have seen many cases where mood and sleep patterns were significantly improved in blocked writers who reconnected with their work in a meaningful way. Some depressed or anxious writers begin writing productively only after they received the appropriate therapy.

Other mental health issues such as bipolar disorder, schizophrenia, post-traumatic stress, grief reactions, and addictions may need to be treated effectively in order for writing to take place. While it is true that some very well-known and prominent writers have had serious mental health disorders, it would be a mistake for the aspiring writer to view a mania, excessive drug use, or alcoholism as the path to boost productivity. The number of talented people who have been rendered incapable of writing due to psychological suffering far exceeds the total of those who have been able to write well in spite of, or because of, their afflictions.

Because writing demands so much of our gray matter, it is also important to keep in mind that brain functioning is a critical factor in both the performance and inner experience of writing. Each writer's brain develops its own unique method of performing and coordinating the many cognitive tasks that are involved. We all have different neurological strengths and challenges, and at the two ends of the continuum there are people who seem to struggle very little with writing and those who struggle a lot. Factors that affect brain functioning such as brain injury, attention deficit disorder, sleep deprivation, and dyslexia increase the challenges significantly. Some authors manage to write productively in spite of such handicaps, but they have to work very hard to do it.

Depression, anxiety, and writing

A thorough exploration of the connections between writing blocks and psychological and neurological disorders is beyond the scope of this book, but it is important to recognize and address these issues if they are part of your writing life.

Subject Matter and Writing Blocks

You may find that your subject matter triggers difficult memories or feelings (for example, writing about a troubled childhood). Moving away from writing in these circumstances is a way of reducing discomfort. Writing is also a powerful social act. If your writing addresses subjects or expresses opinions that breach societal taboos, there are risks involved. The history of literate humanity includes many unfortunate chapters involving book burning and the persecution, imprisonment, and execution of authors whose words have displeased someone. The issues of religion, politics, race, and sex are commonly involved. The death threats made against Salman Rushdie following publication of his book, *The Satanic Verses,* is a good example from the modern era. Even if you do not expect to be lynched or shot for your writing, the anticipation of an angry or rejecting response from the public may generate enough discomfort to block your writing process.

You might also worry about how your writing will affect friends and family. One author in a writing group was stuck for quite a while in her attempts to write a novel because she had drawn on traits of a personal acquaintance in the creation of a rather unpleasant character. Her fear of offending this person stopped her progress for quite some time. She eventually decided to go ahead and write, telling herself it was safe to write whatever she wanted in the privacy of her home and she could decide later about whether it would be a problem to go public with it.

Problems with Success

The prospect of success is challenging to some writers. Psychological issues of this variety sometimes lead to self-sabotaging behaviors connected with feelings of unworthiness or the fear of being the center of attention. I know writers who had early or unanticipated success and could not write after that. A junior professor in one of my groups stalled completely after her first published article landed her a job at a prestigious university. Several elements seemed to have contributed to her paralysis, including fear of being discovered as an imposter and the daunting challenge of matching her initial success.

Self-sabotaging behaviors

It is also important to consider whether anyone important in your life would be threatened, resentful, jealous, or hurt if you were to be successful as a writer. I worked with a young writer who had been blocked for years after her father became enraged and physically threatened her upon learning of her first publishing success. A young professor in a writer's group was blocked on her writing productivity because her husband had been unable to complete his dissertation, and her progress made her feel guilty.

A certain amount of hope and confidence is generally a good thing for a writer, but problems can also arise from the anticipation of a positive public response. A participant in a recent workshop revealed that she became blocked with her writing when she imagined that her book would become an enormous success and she would have to appear on *Oprah*, which terrified her. A grandiose estimation of one's own talents can also lead to blocks in other ways, due to the fear that if the writing is not received with adulation, it will be an injury to one's pride.

Assessing Your Writing Productivity Problems

I like to have as complete an understanding of a person's writing process as possible before I suggest changing anything. This assessment is a tool I created for identifying problems that affect productivity. It highlights a number of issues, habits, thoughts, feelings, and other factors that are commonly associated with writing difficulties. It is a distillation of my observations of struggling writers over the years, and its purpose is to help you target the areas of your writing process that need attention.

Most writers, even those who are content with their level of productivity, will have some or several high scores on this assessment, so don't get upset if you end up with a number of elevated scores. These are helpful in a couple of ways: they highlight the intensity of your relationship with writing and they show you where you can most effectively apply your efforts.

The golden underbelly of a vexatious block is often a powerful desire to write. This tool is not meant to be a scientific instrument for generating diagnostic labels for writers. Use it as a way to deepen your understanding of your writing process and identifying the primary issues to address.

Take a few minutes right now to complete this assessment. Be honest and keep in mind that no one else needs to read your answers, if you choose to keep them private. Pay special attention to any items that trigger emotions, discomfort, confusion, or a desire to shut this book. These items probably point to issues that lie at the heart of your writing challenges, and will help you identify how to best make productive changes.

Writing Productivity Self-Assessment

Rate each question using this scale

Never   Sometimes   Always

1   2   3   4   5

1. **Time**
   - ___ It is hard to find time to write
   - ___ I have too many non-writing professional commitments
   - ___ Other commitments take precedence over writing projects
   - ___ I find it hard to plan my time effectively
   - ___ I resist committing to a regular writing schedule
   - ___ I plan writing time but then do not write
   - ___ Time seems to slip away from me
   - ___ I do not have a good method for prioritizing tasks
   - ___ I don't write without deadline pressure
   - ___ I find it hard to balance writing time with the demands of personal or family relationships

2. **Space**
   - ___ My primary writing space has many distractions in it
   - ___ I am vulnerable to many interruptions where I write
   - ___ My writing space is uncomfortable or inconvenient
   - ___ I have no good place to write
   - ___ My writing space is a dysfunctional mess
   - ___ I avoid writing by cleaning and organizing my space
   - ___ I have equipment or software problems where I write

3. **Starting to write**
   - ___ I have trouble generating good ideas
   - ___ I find it difficult to organize my research or notes
   - ___ I spend too much time reading resource materials
   - ___ I find it hard to create an outline of my projects
   - ___ I "block" when I try to start writing

Bring Your Writing Back to Life!

4. **Procrastination**
   - ___ I consistently avoid writing, though I want to do it
   - ___ I consistently miss goals I set for writing
   - ___ I consistently miss deadlines set by others
   - ___ I daydream or "space out" when I could be writing
   - ___ I criticize myself frequently for procrastinating
   - ___ I conceal from others that I have a problem with procrastination
   - ___ I write in binges when deadlines loom
   - ___ I am dissatisfied with the work I produce when I write in binges
   - ___ I have little or no control over my procrastination

5. **Perfectionism**
   - ___ I feel afraid that others will criticize my work
   - ___ I am very self-critical about my writing
   - ___ I edit first drafts rigorously as I write them
   - ___ The process of writing is painful and slow
   - ___ I rewrite sections repeatedly and still feel dissatisfied
   - ___ I have rigid rules about how the process of writing should go
   - ___ I have a difficult time deciding if my writing is good enough

6. **Difficulty finishing**
   - ___ I spend lots of time researching peripheral issues
   - ___ In major or minor ways, I revise my writing excessively
   - ___ It is difficult for me to decide what to edit out as unnecessary
   - ___ I have multiple unfinished projects; few get done
   - ___ I have difficulty committing fully to my ideas
   - ___ I complete projects but do not submit them

7. **Thinking and feeling patterns connected with writing**

___ Self-criticism	___ Overwhelm	___ Impatience
___ Catastrophizing	___ Resentment	___ Pessimism
___ Arrogance	___ Rebelliousness	___ Dread
___ Imposter feelings	___ Incompetence	___ Fear

THE BLOCKED WRITER'S BOOK OF THE DEAD

8. **Interpersonal issues**
   __ I am reluctant to show my writing to anyone
   __ I have no mentor to advise me about writing
   __ I do not involve other people in my process of writing
   __ I don't know who to seek assistance from if I need it
   __ I feel unsafe acknowledging writing problems to others
   __ My writing productivity is an issue in my personal relationship(s)
   __ I get very upset when others criticize my writing
   __ I have unresolved interpersonal conflicts that affect my productivity
   __ I feel extremely distressed after a manuscript is rejected

9. **Other issues that may affect writing**
   __ Depression
   __ Anxiety/Panic
   __ Grief/Loss
   __ Learning disability, Attention Deficit Disorder
   __ Mental illness (schizophrenia, bipolar disorder, etc.)
   __ Addiction (self or family member)
   __ Life crises or transitions
   __ Writing in a non-native language

Using This Assessment

When you have completed the assessment, review it and note where your scores are:

Highest _____
_____
_____

Lowest _____
_____
_____

Bring Your Writing Back to Life!

These scores will give you a profile of your writing productivity strengths and weaknesses. Below are some recommendations for chapters in the book that will be most relevant for your specific issues.

Time: If you score high on section 1 (Time), then time management will be an important issue to focus on, and you might want to carefully explore Chapters 8 and 9.

Space: High scores on section 2 (Space) of the assessment indicate the presence of the writing space problems addressed in Chapter 7.

Starting: Those of you who score the highest on section 3 (Starting to Write) will probably find Chapters 10–13 to be the most relevant.

Procrastination: Many writers find they score high on section 4 (Procrastination); Chapters 8, 9, and 15 address these issues most directly.

Perfectionism: If you score high in Perfectionism, section 5 of the assessment, Chapters 10–12 will be the most helpful.

Finishing: Section 6 (Difficulty Finishing) high scorers will find useful information in Chapters 8–13.

Thoughts and Feelings: Non-productive thinking and feeling patterns (section 7) are common issues for writers, and Chapters 10 and 11 are the most relevant if you scored high on these items.

Interpersonal: If interpersonal issues (section 8) are an area of concern for you, Chapter 12 should be of assistance.

Other: High scores in section 9 normally indicate a need for additional help beyond the scope offered by this book.

THE BLOCKED WRITER'S BOOK OF THE DEAD

Here are some additional questions to think about:

Are there any issues you had not considered before?
_____
_____
_____

What are the most important areas for you to work on first?
_____
_____
_____

Are there other relevant issues that are not on the list?
_____
_____
_____

Chapter 4

Past Lives and Write Now

Understanding your past as a writer is not always necessary in order to overcome blocks, but it can be an important piece of the process. Your history as a writer is linked to your current writing habits, strengths, fears, and productivity. It may be helpful for you to take a few moments and reflect on your past as a writer and consider how it has affected you. Here are some questions to consider about your personal history as a writer. Jot down some quick responses— you may find it beneficial to discuss them with someone you feel comfortable with and trust.

What are your earliest memories of writing?
_____
_____
_____

What were your experiences and habits of writing during your school years?
_____
_____
_____

When did you realize you wanted to be someone who writes?
_____
_____
_____

THE BLOCKED WRITER'S BOOK OF THE DEAD

Have you experienced writing as being pleasurable in the past? If so, has that changed? When and how did that happen?

_____
_____
_____

Have you had traumatic experiences related to writing? What were they?

_____
_____
_____

When did your difficulties with writing begin? Has writing always been hard or did the difficulties begin at a certain recognizable point in time?

_____
_____
_____

Do you come from a family of writers? If so, how has that helped or hindered your journey as a writer?

_____
_____
_____

What messages, positive or negative, did you receive from family or school about your writing, or about pursuing writing?

_____
_____
_____

What successes have you had as a writer?

_____
_____
_____

Bring Your Writing Back to Life!

Who has helped you with your writing, and who has interfered?

Have you had times when the blocks seemed to recede and you were able to write fluently? If yes, try to reflect upon what might have caused the shift (for example, the influence of another, a change of writing locale, deadline pressure, etc.).

In the process of considering these questions you might recognize connections between your current writing dilemmas and past experiences. See if you can relate your answers to the questions above to your scores on the **Writing Productivity Self-Assessment**.

Blocks are frequently connected to one or a number of previous experiences that have generated connections between painful or aversive memories and writing. In some cases, being able to see and understand these connections can help get things moving again.

The other ghosts from the past that arise consistently in my classes and workshops are linked to educational experiences. Educational institutions are responsible for generating and per-petuating a great many bad habits and teachings about writing. Ignorant and rigid methods of evaluation, unnecessarily destructive judgments and feedback, the encouragement of deadline binge writing, and a lack of sensitivity to different learning styles are education-related issues that can contribute to writer's block.

Your writing process has a history. Be curious and examine it carefully. You may find that learning about your past as a writer is interesting at the very least, and may result in knowledge that is useful for improving your writing productivity.

Chapter 5

The Grateful Blocked

Is it helpful for blocked writers to remember to feel and express gratitude? Is it possible to be blocked as a writer and still feel grateful for your good fortune? Perhaps, though I would not want to minimize the very real suffering and struggle writers often experience. Periods of anguish, as wordless days drag by and deadlines crush in, may make writing feel more like a curse than a blessing.

Most of us take writing for granted as a necessary and fundamental aspect of life and society, but it is actually a fairly recent accomplishment in the history of our species. Even today many of Earth's inhabitants are illiterate. Acquiring the ability to write is a result of good fortune to a large degree. It is a culturally created human capacity that we have inherited from the thousands of previous generations that developed and refined written expression. It is difficult to conceive of the amount of time, energy, creativity, and persistence that millions of people have invested in the project of bringing writing to its present place in human culture. The educational institutions created to develop and pass on this knowledge are now at the heart of our civilization.

Consider the numerous factors that must be present in your life in order to write. First, you need to be born in a culture that already has writers in it, and then be successfully trained over several years to learn how to do it. You need to have reasonably good health, including a brain and nervous system that are functioning well, and you have to have enough financial resources to allow taking time to write. If other life circumstances, relationships, or responsibilities are too problematic or overwhelming, you will not have the time, energy, or concentration that writing demands. In addition, your personality and emotional constitution have to be able to withstand the rigors and challenges of the writing life, and you have to be motivated enough to sustain the effort required. Many of these necessary conditions are not present in the lives of millions on the planet who will never have the opportunity to even consider a life as a writer. You have a chance.

Consider your good fortune

Think for a moment about those who have helped you with writing. Your list might include teachers, parents, living authors, friends, writing colleagues, editors, classmates, reviewers, and others. Your list might also include the literary dead who communicate to you through their works. A sense of appreciation for such blessings can foster a helpful perspective when the writing gets tough. The writing mind can, of course, readily twist blessings into punishment. We can easily get hung up with feeling guilt and self-loathing for not having done more with the gifts we have been given. This is one of many unfortunate mental talents humanity possesses, and it is not likely to help us write. Take a moment to consider your good fortune in being able to write at all, and see if you can then approach your writing as a gift and an opportunity.

Writing Assets, Talents, and Abilities

Before tackling the challenging issues associated with improving writing productivity, remember what you have going for yourself as a writer. It is easy to lose sight of your strong points, or take them for granted when you are focused on what you are not accomplishing. It is these assets that will form the basis of any positive changes, so it

Bring Your Writing Back to Life!

is essential to keep them in mind as key resources and morale aids.

As you review the following list, see what emerges as your chief strengths as a writer. If you identify with only a few items in this list, it doesn't mean things are hopeless. One strong asset may be enough to enable you as a writer. Use the space below the statement to elaborate and give examples for each item; feel free to add to the list if other assets come to mind.

___ I am intelligent
_____

___ I enjoy reading
_____

___ I have perseverance
_____

___ I know my subject well
_____

___ I have passion for my subject
_____

___ I enjoy writing
_____

___ I have a good memory
_____

___ I have a broad vocabulary
_____

___ I know grammar
_____

THE BLOCKED WRITER'S BOOK OF THE DEAD

___ I have an effective writing style

___ I can entertain with words

___ I have a good imagination

___ I am well organized

___ I have good quantitative skills

___ I collaborate well with others

___ I have good typing skills

___ I've had success with writing

___ I have a sense of humor

___ I have good research skills

___ I have a desire to share knowledge

Bring Your Writing Back to Life!

___ I have a strong work ethic

___ I can persuade people

___ I am able to reason logically

___ I am able to tell a good story

___ I love language and words

___ I have supportive friends and/or family

___ I have helpful mentors and/or peers

___ I have good computer skills

Other assets, talents, and abilities:

As you review the items you have noted as strengths, try to identify those capabilities that you rely on when you write. You may take some of these strengths for granted or consider them unimportant, but they are important and you draw from them when you write. There may have been a time when you faced a tough project and succeeded, or when someone offered you very useful advice, which you accepted, applied, and benefited from. Think about how these strengths can assist you now, and how you can stay connected with them.

Chapter 6

Motivations for Writing

On the final day of a recent class, one participant thanked me profusely and shared that she was very pleased with the progress she had made. She had been avoiding and agonizing over an article for months and during the class she decided to just abandon it completely. After that she felt much, much happier. I'm still unsure whether I ought to consider this as a success or a failure of my methods, but it did cause me to reflect about the question: "Why do people bother to write at all?"

As should be apparent by now, the barriers and challenges to writing are many and powerful. This means there must be sufficient motivation for us to undertake the effort to write in an ongoing way. I encourage you to identify your motives and evaluate the importance of writing in your life. Many writers consider writing to be a highly important activity that gives their lives considerable meaning and satisfaction. In general I find that writers are much happier when they are writing regularly and productively. This observation has reinforced my desire to work with blocked writers, who are often unhappy, because I really enjoy seeing their mood improve.

Why do you want to write? There are as many answers to this question as there are people who write. Below is a list of some common motivators for writing. It is not exhaustive, but you might want to note the items that apply to you, and add others that aren't on the list. Review the ones you identify with and note how important or meaningful each one is to you. Getting clear about your motivation(s) and the importance of writing in your life might serve to enhance your commitment to actually doing it. How important is writing compared to other aspects of living that you engage in? Without sufficient desire it is hard to muster the energy to face the challenges writing entails. Perhaps your desire is strong but you ignore or repress it. You may be only partially unaware of how important writing is to you. Staying in touch with your motivation will assist you in sustaining your commitment to the ongoing practice of writing.

Bring Your Writing Back to Life!

Motivations for Writing

Rate each item and add specific thoughts where relevant

Weak Motivator ---------- Strong Motivator

    1   2   3   4   5

___ To achieve educational goals

_____

___ To sell something

_____

___ To achieve professional goals

_____

___ To stimulate change

_____

___ To contribute to a field of knowledge

_____

___ Creative expression

_____

___ To answer a question or solve a problem

_____

___ To entertain

_____

THE BLOCKED WRITER'S BOOK OF THE DEAD

___ To investigate situations and reveal facts

___ To make money

___ Personal reflection and growth

___ For enjoyment of the process

___ To build a reputation and gain recognition

___ To help people

___ To take on a challenge

___ To rebel or provoke

___ To enjoy people's reactions

___ To influence or persuade

___ Answering an inner drive to write

Bring Your Writing Back to Life!

___ To tell a story

___ To fulfill someone else's expectations

___ I don't know

Others: _____
_____
_____

Review what you have rated and written, and reflect on your motivations for writing. If your motivation level is high, you probably experience the state of being blocked or non-productive as very distressing. You will need to reconnect with your writing to ease that pain, and keeping your motivators in mind will help you do that.

Chapter 7

A Room, Womb, or Tomb of One's Own

"If, however, o nobly born, thou hast, because of the influence of karma, to enter into a womb, the teaching for the selection of the womb door will be explained now. Listen."

~ *The Tibetan Book of the Dead*

The earliest writings included in *The Egyptian Book of the Dead* were originally chiseled in stone in the tombs of deceased pharaohs and royalty. Tomb size, quality, furnishings, and decoration were all considered critical for determining the spirit's fate in the afterworld, so careful consideration and planning were involved. The scribes responsible for carving the hieroglyphics had considerable status in their culture, but they undoubtedly endured adversities such as poor lighting, lousy ventilation, annoying co-workers, ergonomically incorrect work stations, and repetitive stress injuries. Their writing blocks were made out of granite. (No wonder their daily word count was so low!) We are fortunate to live in an age when more amenable settings and tools for writing exist.

Having a good enough place to do your writing is important, even if it doesn't guarantee that any writing will occur there. Indeed, many ideal locations lie fallow season after season as their inhabitants languish in the numerous psychological purgatories and hells reserved for those called to the writing life. Nevertheless, you can at least improve your odds of writing more productively by choosing and arranging your work setting in a thoughtful fashion. Your writing place should be accessible, functional, and comfortable enough so that at the very least it does not contribute to work problems or avoidance.

The Tibetan Book of the Dead has specific instructions for souls approaching a rebirth into the earthly plane of existence. These teachings are instructions for identifying desirable and undesirable wombs to enter. It is emphasized that this choice has enormous consequences on the practical and spiritual success of one's next life, and should be approached in an informed and careful way. A writer's place of work is like a womb in that gestation, growth, labor, and birth occur in both, so perhaps modern writers should pay heed to the spirit of these ancient teachings.

To help you evaluate how well your room, womb, or tomb is serving you, consider the following questions.

Is it easy for you to get to your writing space, or are there practical or psychological barriers that interfere?

Some people work best with a dedicated writing zone that is not used for other activities. It is less complicated and easier to start working if you do not have to do a lot of preliminary arranging of your space before getting down to it. When I was learning to play guitar, I found I was much more likely to practice if the guitar was out on the stand. If I had to contemplate the additional steps of locating the case, opening it, and removing the guitar, I was much less likely to play. It seems idiotic that something this trivial could make a difference, but perhaps this type of idiocy is our lot, and we should learn how to best live with it.

Do you have any negative feelings about the place itself?

Do negative feelings about your writing place ever deter you from beginning or continuing to work? Are you comfortable enough in the place where you usually write? Are there any disturbing environmental issues such as temperature problems, poor lighting, distracting noises, bad furniture, or noxious odors? Is the room depressing, claustrophobic, or too messy? Can any of these conditions be improved without great effort or expense? Does your writing space need to be cleaned up or reorganized? Is that a task you also avoid? When a general cleaning is in order, I encourage you to resist doing it during your writing time.

Evaluating your writing place

How frequently do interruptions and distractions occur, and what specifically are they?

Convincingly valid interruptions can, of course, be readily self-generated in any location, but some settings will put you at greater risk. Do people pop in and talk to you uninvited? Are you likely to be called away to solve someone else's pressing problems during your writing time? Is the phone an issue? Do you secretly feel grateful for these interruptions? Interruptions are a problem for many writers, both at the office and at home. There is no life without interruptions, but putting in a bit of effort to minimize them during your writing time should pay off. For example, you can close your door, inform people that you'd like to be left alone, and silence your phone.

If you write at work, are your attempts to write defeated by the demands of non-writing tasks?

The temptation to engage in other professional activities (or perhaps even quasi-professional activities) readily undermines the discipline for writing. This issue arises frequently for academics who have colleagues and students seeking their attention on the job. A professor I know put a "Do Not Disturb!" sign on her door while writing, and then trained those in her environment to respect it and hold their questions until her writing hour was over. Others find that writing in the office early in the morning or in the evening works well because so few other people are around. Putting the phone on voice mail and postponing the urge to check e-mail during writing times are good habits to initiate. If all efforts fail and distractions prevail, it may be the case that the office is not a good place for you to write.

Do you write at home?

Writing at home has advantages as well as risks. Family influences and distractions can be powerful barriers to writing productivity. Is there sufficient privacy and quiet to allow concentration? Are there children or significant others who might be seeking your attention or resenting you for sequestering yourself in your room? Are there unfinished home projects and tasks that will compete with writing for your attention? How do you maintain your resolve to write when hobbies, hot baths, television, and food are so readily available?

How isolated do you need to be to focus on your work?

There are those writers who find the ambience and background noise of a café beneficial; others need complete privacy and silence. Do you relish the aloneness that often accompanies writing, or does it give you the creeps? Is music or background noise a help or a hindrance?

Is your writing space supplied with whatever materials, computers, books, and other writing tools you need so you don't have to get up in search of essentials?

Each time you rise up to roam around looking for something, you are increasing the chances that when you sit down again it will be in a chair in another galaxy far, far away from your project.

Do you write in more than one place?

Writing in more than one place may open additional opportunities to be productive, though there are potential risks and hassles. If you use two computers, make sure the programs are compatible so your work can be integrated. Transferring sections back and forth can lead to errors and mishaps. Laptops provide the convenience of working virtually anywhere, though they need to be backed up regularly in case of disk crashes, loss, or theft. Laptops provide mobility and the flexibility to write in numerous locations and make use of free chunks of time when you are away from your usual workspace, but long typing stints on the laptop are rougher on the neck, arms, and eyes. Any computer station that leads to repetitive stress injuries will greatly reduce your productivity, so ergonomic considerations are important.

What about using the computer?

This wonderful invention offers many improvements over typewriters and chisels in terms of accelerating the writing process, but it is a double-edged sword. Computers provide easy access to tempting, time-gobbling distractions such as e-mail, Web surfing, instant messaging, and games, games, games, games. Do any of these activities affect your productivity? If so, consider ways to reduce exposure to these temptations. A professor I worked with decided to have two desks and two computers in his office. One set-up was for writing and the second was for all other tasks related to his job. His writing computer was not connected to the Internet and all games had been removed. The effort required to stand up, cross the room, and turn on the other system was a sufficient deterrent to his passion for engaging in cyberspace distractions. Those who avoid writing by playing computer games (boring and mindless games like solitaire are usually chosen for this purpose) are often initially reluctant when I ask them to delete the games from their computer. At the very least, try to make them harder to get to. An effective general rule to employ is to always *write first*, before diving into the vast oceans of entertainment the computer provides.

Write first

Should you change where you write?

A writing space that has been the site of long-standing struggle and repeated disappointment can itself become haunted like a tomb—evoking memories that trigger negative feelings and habits of avoidance. If this is your situation, no matter how perfect the spot may appear, you might want to experiment with going somewhere else to see what happens. I have had several people tell me that after making a change of locale they found a renewed energy and interest in regular writing. For the same reason that it sometimes works to just kick a malfunctioning soda machine, this geographical remedy occasionally works with writing blocks, though additional measures are generally required to effect a lasting change. The important thing is to notice how you feel and how well you work in your chosen setting, and then to improve it if you need to.

Both wombs and tombs are launching pads for entry into another world. The ancient books of the dead emphasize the need to pay attention, make good decisions, and prepare properly to ensure a successful journey. As you prepare to launch into writing, make sure your pad is made of the right stuff.

Chapter 8

House-Training the Writer Within

"O nobly-born, (so and so), listen.
That thou art suffering so cometh from
thine own karma; it is not due to anyone else's:
it is thine own karma."
> ~ *The Tibetan Book of the Dead*

Each time you put off working on your article, poem, or novel, you create a moment of relief for yourself. It feels good to procrastinate because (for a while, anyway) you don't have to face the many challenges that writing presents. Unfortunately, this works like house-training a new puppy by giving him a biscuit when he pees on the rug instead of on the paper. There is an experience of some immediate, welcome relief but what follows is a mess you have to clean up later. Typically such patterns are repeated and reinforced, which causes you to procrastinate again and again, despite your best intentions.

Counterproductive writing habits die hard. The writers attending my classes have often struggled with the same problem or set of problems for years and are often quite discouraged. After repeated experiences of failure, the feelings of powerlessness, hopelessness, frustration, overwhelm, and self-loathing take root in the psyche. It is natural to want to avoid going through these uncomfortable internal experiences again and again, so a variety of psychological

THE BLOCKED WRITER'S BOOK OF THE DEAD

Procrastination operates like heroin

and behavioral tactics arise that provide some measure of relief by interfering with writing. Procrastination operates like a heroin addiction: it fixes our immediate discomfort while leading us into hell.

If your bad habits have been long-standing, then you are probably not fully aware of the mechanisms that control your behavior. You may not consciously register the fact that you are automatically re-enacting a pattern of avoidance behavior designed (by you) to protect you from an uncomfortable experience or feeling. Daydreaming, forgetfulness, rationalizing, confusion, and getting distracted by less-crucial tasks are all aspects of this cycle. Habits are resilient and efforts toward change must be carefully considered and executed in order to be successful.

The first step is to study your writing habits as specifically and objectively as possible, with a spirit of curiosity and self-forgiveness. Focus on how you behave day to day, as you respond to the following questions.

Make a list of the things you typically do when you are avoiding writing.

_____
_____
_____

Do you reward yourself for not writing in any obvious or subtle way? How?

_____
_____
_____

Bring Your Writing Back to Life!

Do you do anything that makes writing unappealing or aversive?

Some part of you will experience efforts to increase productivity as threatening, aggravating, or an imposition. You need to address this inner conflict skillfully in order to overcome this challenge. A man in one of my groups described his process of changing habits as "tiptoeing past a sleeping lion." Keep moving forward without waking up the hungry beast of resistance.

One approach for altering writing habits based on principles from behavioral psychology is useful to consider. These principles come from research into methods for altering human behavior. The goal is to reinforce the desired behavior (writing) and discourage unwanted behavior (avoiding writing).

Here are some of these strategies that I have found to work.

1. Stack the deck in your favor
2. Make a work schedule and track performance
3. Break big projects into specific, realizable tasks with short time frames
4. Identify and remove rewards for unwanted behavior
5. Decrease exposure to temptations and distractions
6. Harness your neuroses
7. Make a routine, simple pleasure contingent upon writing first
8. Reinforce success

Make failure less likely

A woman in my class complained that this behavioral approach incorporates the same techniques scientists use to teach rats to press levers for food pellets. I had to concede the point, but later found it gratifying to learn that she had developed the routine of rewarding herself with one M&M (a pellet of sorts) for every page she wrote.

Stack the deck in your favor

I encourage blocked writers to make failure less likely to occur. For many reasons writing is frequently difficult to do, so respect that reality and set yourself up as well as possible to succeed. Protect yourself from habitual tendencies that predictably derail your train of words.

If you have identified factors that have helped you write successfully in the past, incorporate these elements into your preparations and planning for your writing sessions. This could be as simple as recreating the same writing space you had when you wrote well in the past. If someone really helped you with a previous successful project, is that person or someone similar available now?

Make changes by taking small steps that would be very difficult to *not* do. For instance, if your goal is to start writing every day, if you make the sessions short (15 minutes) you may find it hard to rationalize skipping the session. I encourage you to be pragmatic and do what works, whether or not it fits your image of what a "real" writer would do. Here are some ideas to experiment with.

Make a Work Schedule

⊙ *Write daily.*

This could mean Monday through Friday. A seven-day schedule can also work if the writer's life is not already out of balance from overworking. Writing at the same time each day helps to strengthen the habit. This is impossible for many writers, but you can strive to make the weekly routine as consistent as possible. An advantage of a regular schedule is that it eliminates the daily process of *deciding* when to write. Each time you have to make a decision about writing, it increases the likelihood that you will decide not to do it. The more regularly you write, the less dreadful it feels to face it each day. To the extent that you generate new, positive associations with writing through regular practice, you reinforce your efforts. I have met many writers who hate scheduling their writing and refuse to do it. Some believe that working with a schedule is a worthy idea, but they have never been able to stick to one. Scheduling writing is not the only way to become more productive, but I have seen it produce powerful results for those blocked writers who found a way to move in this direction. Write daily. Write daily. Write daily. This is the single most important piece of advice in this book.

⊙ *If work avoidance is a problem, begin with short writing periods.*

The goal to strive for initially is the establishment of new routines, not an amazing daily word count. The initiation of a routine of regular writing sessions will predictably generate some uncomfortable feelings, and these are easier to tolerate if the period is brief. If you have been doing little or no writing, 15 minutes may be a good time period to set aside when you begin. One blocked writer complained to me that 15 minutes was not long enough because he was already so far behind on his project. I asked how much writing he was currently doing each day. When he said, "None," I asked if 15 minutes would be better than that. He looked irritated, but he did stop complaining.

Establish a routine

   Those who experiment with short sessions often find that more gets done in those few minutes than they might have guessed. But the real advantage of the short sessions is the establishment of a consistent practice of writing. You can increase the duration later when the habit becomes stronger.

◉ *Choose a time when your energy is good and distractions will be minimal.*

Many people find writing to be hard work that requires their best concentration and energy level. Mornings are frequently a good time for that, with an added benefit being that the work is done early and you don't have to think about it for the rest of the day. But mornings are unavailable for many people with families and jobs. A scientist in one of my groups had to work in her lab every morning, so she began the routine of writing her papers in the late afternoon, just before she went home. It wasn't perfect because she had lower energy at that point, but it was beneficial because her experimental work was fresh in her mind and everyone else had left by then.

If you have a plan to write early but then postpone the work for later in the day, you greatly increase the odds that nothing will happen. If you have this postponing habit, I recommend you adopt the rule that you *have* to wait until the next day to write if you miss your scheduled time. This spares you the stress of disappointing yourself day after day, and it implicitly communicates that writing is a privilege rather than a burden.

For those who come alive after sundown, the advantages of late-night writing might include a quiet house and fewer interruptions and distractions. Sometimes jobs, families, and other obligations will unavoidably suck up your best energy, and you have to make the most of whatever time is left, with whatever energy you have.

Bring Your Writing Back to Life!

◉ *Resist the urge to overdo it.*

When a surge of energy for writing rolls in, it's tempting to ride the wave until it crashes. If you get too excited, however, and press far into the wee hours, sleep is lost and energy, concentration, and the desire to write will be less available the next day. Heroically long writing sessions are hard to sustain day after day and can lead to feelings of burnout that interfere with motivation. Even if you feel like you are on a roll, it may be best to stop and make a note of the ideas you wish to address as the starting point for the next session. This step will help bring closure to your work for the day, allow time for rest, and create momentum for starting up again.

◉ *Track your performance.*

Make a chart for the refrigerator, keep a writing journal, or put a gold star on your calendar when you have written. Small efforts add up over time and it is encouraging to see progress when you review your writing record. The act of regularly recording your writing efforts tends to promote productivity by consistently bringing your attention to the issue. In my experience most blocked writers don't follow this recommendation because it calls forth the same avoidance impulses that writing does, and is depressing to do when writing is not happening. It somehow makes me feel I am doing my job properly when I recommend performance tracking, even if only a handful of people ever do it. If you are serious about wanting to change your writing habits, experiment with this.

Break Big Projects into Bite-Sized Chunks

I like the word "chunks." It reminds me of those wonderful bricks of chocolate that break down into six or eight smaller blocks. For

Maintaining your focus

writers it means breaking off a chunk of work each day that is small enough to swallow. It is wise to resist the temptation to fixate on the unfathomable enormity of attempting to write a *book* or a *dissertation*. Such thoughts generate anxiety, confusion, and a sense of being overwhelmed. For instance, long-distance open-water swimmers use a technique of lifting their heads and looking forward toward their destination with every fifth or sixth breath. Their other breaths are taken by rotating the head to the side, which requires less energy and maintains speed better. Looking at the finish line with every breath is exhausting and slows one down because it puts the body in the wrong position in the water. This is a model that writers can consider: take a sighting on the whole project occasionally to stay on track, but focus on the daily goals and tasks most of the time. And keep breathing.

For writers who do not plan projects but create them as they go using a more intuitive process, breaking a project into segments might not work. In these cases the bite-sized chunks might be the chunks of time they commit to their writing each day. Do the daily minutes of writing and trust that the larger project will fall into place over time.

Identify and Remove Rewards for Unwanted Behavior

If you love sweets and you head for the cookie jar when you should be writing, keep in mind that eating that cookie will make it harder for you to write tomorrow. It is more than just being a little naughty; you are conditioning your behavior to thwart your own aspirations. The cookie might not taste so sweet if you look at it this way. Sometimes it is hard to even identify how you are reinforcing your own unwanted habits. Those of you who scrub tile grout to avoid writing may not recognize that there is some element of relief or self-reward involved in that activity, but there is.

Decrease Exposure to Temptations and Distractions

Choose a time and place to write that will limit your contact with anything associated with your most common avoidance behaviors. These behaviors are usually identifiable, and by making a conscious decision to get out of harm's way, you increase the odds that you'll write. Food, television, the phone, reading material, computer games, e-mail, Web surfing, and socializing are common distracting factors; making them less accessible when you write is one way to stack the deck in your favor.

Harness Your Neuroses

A doctoral student in one of my groups was eventually able to finish her dissertation by telling her department secretary that she would give her one page of the document every day. She knew that walking into the department without that page would create unbearable shame and embarrassment for her, so she overcame her resistance and produced. Another class participant would schedule times for doing housecleaning, which she hated, because then she would write in order to avoid doing those chores. Faced with two bad alternatives, we choose the less aversive. People often ask me why the predictable, long-term negative consequences of not writing—like guilt, self-loathing, and regret—won't motivate them to write. I tell them it's because the immediate relief of procrastinating in the moment is a more powerful factor for determining behavior than the anticipation of some bad feelings in the future.

Make a Routine, Simple Pleasure Contingent Upon Writing First

This might mean you would not read the newspaper, check your e-mail, watch television, or talk on the phone until some minimum amount of writing has taken place. Choose something that is part of your daily life that is somewhat pleasurable. One doctoral student I worked with was getting quite good at the piano during a several-month period when he did no work on his dissertation. By making piano playing contingent on his having written each day, he was able to establish a regular writing regime and finish the project. This tactic also reinforces the writing habit because the work is followed with a reward.

Reinforce Success

If you follow a successful work session with something pleasant, you will be building a positive association that supports your good writing habits. I've known writers who have developed post-writing routines involving meals, naps, music, light reading, or socializing. If you are like most writers I've known, the most powerful reward for reinforcing your writing habit is seeing the fruits of your labor in the form of completed pages. An additional reward biscuit is often not necessary, but if you give yourself one anyway, you will enjoy it all the more knowing your writing for the day is done.

Do not try to incorporate all of these bits of advice into your writing life

Experiment with one or two approaches at first. Start small and proceed gradually. The goal at this point is not to produce reams of text; it is to *create new habits*. The increase in production will follow naturally. You can change your writing karma.

Chapter 9

Procrastination: The Sickness Unto Deadline

"O procrastinating one, who thinketh not of the coming of death,
Devoting thyself to the useless doings of this life,
Improvident art thou in dissipating thy great opportunity;
Mistaken, indeed, will thy purpose be now if thou returnest
empty-handed (without having written) from this life:
Since the Holy Dharma (writing) is known to be thy true need,
Wilt thou not devote thyself to the Holy Dharma (writing)
even now?"

~ *The Tibetan Book of the Dead* (parentheses mine)

Procrastination is one of the enduring challenges of human experience and behavior. It is viewed in American culture as a moral failing and is often equated with sloth, one of the seven deadly sins. Writers who procrastinate may castigate themselves for being "lazy," but that label is misleading. Laziness implies a degree of contented relaxation that rarely applies to writers. The procrastination state is typically very dynamic and uncomfortable on the inside, even if nothing is happening on the outside.

On page 67 is a visual depiction of the process of procrastination that I created using the patterns I most frequently encounter with writers. It is based loosely on the Buddhist "Wheel of Samsara," which depicts the cyclic, self-perpetuating nature of human suffering. While everyone's style of procrastination is unique, several common features are included in this wheel. The point of presenting the issue in this way is to highlight how we unwittingly create and maintain behavior that we don't like, and then feel unhappy and controlled by it. The more times we go around the wheel, the more we reinforce the pattern. The steps become grooved and automatic, and the wheel eventually spins without our conscious awareness. If this cycle seems familiar to you, you are not alone.

Unwittingly reinforcing bad habits

It is useful to imagine that you have more than one "will" controlling the decisions you make, and that some of these "wills" have their own agendas that are at odds with the writing goals you have set. The other wills need to be acknowledged and contended with thoughtfully and skillfully. They are not stupid and in fact have made a career out of gaining control and outsmarting other intentions that might lead to discomfort. We can view such psychological mechanisms as self-protection programs that have become too effective. That is because we have reinforced them continually over the years. We feel victimized and powerless because we don't see that we are also the perpetrator.

Let's take a spin around the procrastination wheel and examine the issues.

⊙ *Unclear, Unrealistic Goals; Denial of the Problem*

Even when there has been a consistent, enduring pattern of work avoidance in the past, it is common for procrastinators to be naively hopeful and optimistic before embarking on a writing project. It is a form of denial about the problem. In your mind it seems that it should be fairly easy to tackle the project, and you dismiss any inner voices warning you about long-standing avoidance patterns. You might say to yourself, "This time I'll just write every day and stay ahead of the deadlines. No more of that procrastination wheel for

Bring Your Writing Back to Life!

Procrastination
The Wheel of Suffering

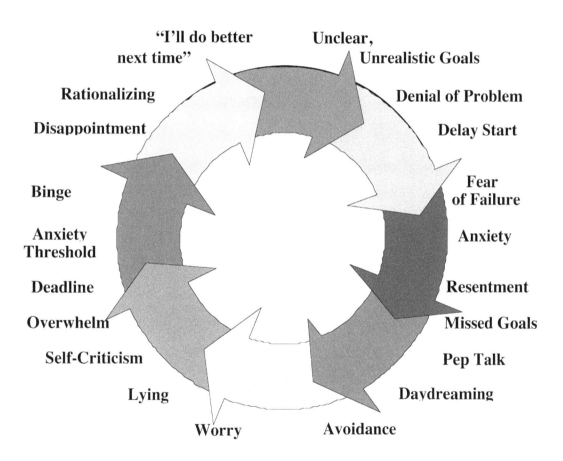

me!" This denial has the consequence of interfering with the need to be thoughtful about managing your behavior. If you tell yourself that writing should go easily, then why should you bother making plans about potential problems? So you get out of the gate poorly prepared to meet the predictably difficult challenges that lie ahead. You are also blindly stepping onto the wheel of procrastination by laying the groundwork for delaying the start of writing.

One method of working with this issue is to acknowledge that you have a problem. Completing and reviewing the Writing Productivity Self-Assessment is one way to determine the nature and severity of your problem. This may sting the pride or generate feelings such as shame, overwhelm, and dread, but if such problems exist, it's best to face them. If you accept that your patterns of work avoidance *will always recur,* then you can realistically put some plans in place for diminishing their impact. An example of this sort of planning will be presented in the final chapter of this book, "Your Writing Productivity Improvement Plan."

⊙ *Delay Start*

Time seems plentiful at the very beginning of a writing project. There seems to be no big problem with letting things slide a bit. "What's the hurry?" There is usually some physical and emotional comfort connected with this postponing, and it is easy to quiet that tiny voice of truth inside that is encouraging you to get started, because there is seemingly such a large cushion of time. "I'll get to it soon enough—don't worry!" This is the top of the slippery slope, and without knowing it, you are setting up the dynamics for the rest of the project, which is the pattern of avoiding writing.

It helps at this point on the wheel to remember the command "Write first!" This means that no matter what your inner dialogue is telling you, the best way to proceed is to do the more challenging task (writing) before you do *anything* else. Even if you work for only five minutes, you will start the project by writing rather than postponing, and this is the right formula for improved productivity. Beginning this way will also make it easier to start work the next day and the day after.

⊙ *Fear of Failure; Anxiety*

As time passes you feel the need to get going and at this point you might experience tendrils of fear working their way into your consciousness. It begins to dawn that the task facing you may be more difficult than you previously admitted to yourself. As you imagine beginning to write, anxiety starts to percolate. Self-doubts about your competence arise, memories of previous failures surface, and a sense of dread engulfs you. One of the problems with anxiety is that it interferes with concentration and short-term memory, both of which are essential to writing. As a result, attempts to write at this point might be false starts, reinforcing your fear that you will not succeed. It feels better to distract and calm yourself by popping open a beer or checking your Facebook page. The **Wheel of Suffering** gains momentum.

Anxiety interferes with concentration and memory

⊙ *Resentment*

As discomfort and stress register more clearly in your mind and body, you feel trapped. You wonder how you ever got yourself into such a hell. You want to strike out and slug someone, but there really is no one to blame. Your resentment might make you rebel against writing, rip up drafts, bristle at friends and family, mentally flagellate yourself, and kick your dog. Sometimes this resentment takes the rebellious form of "No one tells *me* what to do; not even *myself*!"

Resentment and fear are close relatives, and in the chapter "Feelings" I will explore in greater detail how to approach working

Convert negative emotions into fuel

with emotions so they have less effect on productivity. One key is building the skill of continuing to write even when these feelings emerge. When you are emotionally worked up, it is easy to tell yourself that writing is too hard, or that you are in the wrong mood for writing. You will benefit from learning how to gently lean into your work even when anger and fear are present. It is helpful to remember that all feelings are temporary and pass with time. Sometimes these emotional energies can be converted to fuel and channeled into the writing in a useful way.

⊙ *Missed Goals: Pep Talks*

Now that the pattern of postponing has been established and your inner turmoil is activated, you attempt to establish goals for productivity to bring yourself to the task. As in the first stage of the **Wheel of Suffering**, you are still in denial about the seriousness of the problem. You attempt to address the powerful forces of procrastination by generating some inner deadlines, writing them on your calendar, and giving yourself pep talks about why you should get going. The humbling reality is that these attempts to resolve the problem are ineffective, and you cannot make yourself sit down at your desk and type on the keyboard by simply telling yourself that you should.

⊙ *Daydreaming*

Daydreaming is truly a tricky problem. When you daydream you disconnect from awareness of your immediate life in this world and slip into a realm where your mind drifts along on other currents. In the morning you might give yourself the goal of writing five pages before breakfast but somehow, three hours later, you find yourself in the grocery store buying chocolate chip cookies and renting a DVD. Your mind is not your own. The process of disconnecting and getting lost in the labyrinths of the mind is subtle and quick. You are usually unaware that it is happening.

If this is one of your challenges, it is useful to have external structures and reminders for your writing life. This may mean discussing your writing process with other people who will hold you accountable and encourage you. You can arrange to meet and write with others, if that helps. Classes and critique groups also provide a regular external structure for focusing on your writing, and the thought of arriving at an upcoming session with nothing to show is often a strong motivation to stay on task.

It also helps to have dedicated writing periods scheduled in your day and written on your calendar or posted on your refrigerator. You might also set up cues such as buzzers on your iPhone© that go off to remind you to write, etc. Even when we remember to write, within minutes of beginning your mind may wander. Writing often brings up stressful feelings, so the impulse to wander about in the recesses of your inner mind is seductive because it allows relief. When you allow your consciousness to be captured by unconscious forces within you, you lose valuable time and become unproductive.

Mindfulness meditation is another good practice for strengthening your connection with the reality from which you write. This is a meditation practice that cultivates awareness of the present moment. Mindfulness practices developed from Buddhism described in John Kabot-Zinn's book *Full Catastrophe Living* and Jack Kornfield's *A Path with Heart* are simple, effective ways to improve concentration, awareness of the moment, and openness to whatever arises—all of these skills are useful to writers.

◉ *Avoidance; Worry*

As you travel around the **Wheel of Suffering**, your level of concern escalates, as does your motivation to avoid. Worry is a good thing on one hand because it elevates your awareness of what you need to do, but it is also uncomfortable, so it simultaneously amplifies the impulse to avoid writing. You may witness yourself engaging in self-sabotaging behavior, yet be unable to stop procrastinating. The level of distress associated with your project dips *temporarily* each time you avoid writing, but your internal payload of discomfort continues to grow and weigh on you more and more. There seems to be no way out except to worry more and avoid more.

◉ *Lying; Self-Criticism*

Now that a good bit of time has passed with not enough to show for it, shame and self-loathing worm their way into your psyche. If you are asked about your writing, it feels too embarrassing to tell the truth, so you hedge a bit, or maybe a lot. You tell your friends, teachers, colleagues, or significant others that you are making progress, even though you really aren't. You may also delude yourself that the situation is different than it really is. At this point you feel badly about both your inability to write and the fact that you are deceiving others. More bad feelings now become associated with writing, making it just that much more onerous to sit down and face the monster. In addition, you are now carrying the fear that some of the people you lied to will find out the truth, resulting in the possibility of painful relationship damage. You sometimes wonder how you will ever get out of your predicament, and your stress level rises. You feel out of control.

◉ *Overwhelm; Deadline; Anxiety Threshold*

As the final deadline for completing your project becomes imminent, reality breaks through and you become motivated by dread and fear of failure. As this fear of failure becomes more powerful than the fear of facing your writing, you are propelled into desperate action. You imagine the awful consequences of not completing your work on time, and are genuinely baffled about how you could have put yourself in this predicament again. You had promised yourself you would not wait until the last minute to begin, but you did. Now, however, there is no time for wallowing in self-pity, daydreaming, or lecturing yourself. Somehow you have to do it, and even though the challenge seems monumental, you force yourself to face the task.

Deadline-driven writing frenzy

◉ *Binge; Disappointment; Rationalizing*

At this point on the **Wheel of Suffering**, a last-minute, deadline-driven frenzy of writing erupts. With or without the use of stimulants of various sorts, long binges of work ensue in an adrenalized state of hyperactivity. Everything else in life is sidelined and forgotten as the monomaniacal focus on writing takes center stage. You might feel both dread and thrill in trying to beat the clock and perhaps a perverse sense of satisfaction that you were able to procrastinate for so long and yet will still be able to complete the project.

Generally, if you finish in this way, you know you could have done a better job if you had not been forced to write in a manic binge. There may be a sense of disappointment in either the final product, yourself, or both. After this disappointment comes the ego-assuaging mental exercise where you tell yourself that you really are more capable than the writing shows, and that you could have done better if you had had sufficient time. You might come up with other rationalizations that explain why things turned out the way they did.

⊙ *"I'll Do Better Next Time"*

This is the juncture where, after the work is completed, you make a promise to yourself to change how you approach your writing. You know it would be better to not procrastinate and mentally, you reaffirm your commitment to this goal. The problem is that you leave out the implementation of a clear and defined path to accomplish these non-trivial changes in your behavior. Somehow you feel it is enough to simply tell yourself that it will be different next time. But it isn't. You start another journey around the wheel.

Quick-fix solutions are ineffective

I always ask writers who procrastinate what they have previously done to try to overcome the problem. Often the reply is "Nothing" or a variation of "I tell myself I shouldn't procrastinate" or "I get mad at myself." Sometimes I hear "I've tried everything," but this is never true. When you are spinning on the wheel it is hard to think creatively, even to see obvious solutions. You may know what will help, but find you are unable to do it. Attempted "solutions" such as internal pep talks and verbal self-flagellation only perpetuate the pattern instead of altering it. In my classes I gently try to communicate the message that these approaches don't work for a very good reason. *They are completely inadequate*. You need sharper arrows in your quiver to slay the dragon of procrastination. Quick-fix solutions to long-standing procrastination patterns are as effective as fad diets, especially if those solutions are part of the wheel itself (e.g., self-criticism, unrealistic plans, binge writing at deadlines, internal pep talks).

You can jump off the **Wheel of Suffering** at any point in the cycle. It is important to remember to respect the power of these patterns, and to set expectations and goals accordingly. Any action you take to get off, slow down, or stop the wheel will call forth resistance. The resistance may be an unconscious veering away from the project, a cascade of frightening or dreadful thoughts, a vague but compelling feeling of dread, or a deviously well-crafted rationalization for doing nothing. You can learn to recognize the resistance in the form of the non-productive thoughts, feelings, and behavior patterns that you've identified in your Writing Productivity Self-Assessment. If you are aware of your resistance as it occurs in the moment, you have the option of choosing to write in spite of it. This is easier said than done, and we never succeed 100 percent of the time, but every tiny victory serves to slow the cycle.

Begin with small steps that are only mildly uncomfortable, because feelings of anxiety, overwhelm, resentment, and dread are more likely to be activated if our goals and expectations are too ambitious. The best way to break the cycle at any point is to go ahead and write a little bit every day, even if some inner voice is screaming at you to pop a beer and turn on the TV. This takes some effort, but afterward you will feel good knowing that you have established some control over the process.

Chapter 10

Not in Your Write Mind
Thoughts and Feelings about Writing

"O nobly-born, whatever fearful and terrifying visions thou mayest see recognize them to be thine own thought forms."

~ *The Tibetan Book of the Dead*

Humanity has been graced with an exquisite brain, frequently touted as the crowning achievement of evolution. Because of this biological marvel, our species has distinguished itself among living organisms by developing, among other things, the complex skills of reading and writing. In fact, in the rather brief period that humankind has been able to read and write, astounding and vast literary traditions have been established on our once-illiterate planet. The thinking brain has truly been a blessing to our species, but it comes with a dark side. We have a mind with a depth and complexity so magnificent that it is also capable of thoroughly undermining our attempts to engage in the wonderful enterprise of writing. Our remarkable, mischievous mind is both our staunchest ally and wiliest adversary in the writing process.

In *The Tibetan Book of the Dead,* the entire post-mortem adventure is understood as a grand projection of our own mental processes. Numerous passages exhort the departed soul to remember the illusory nature of experiences in the afterlife, and to not be afraid or deceived by these confused beliefs and visions of the mind. This is also good advice for blocked writers. If disturbing or distracting thoughts are interfering with your ability to sit down and write, then it makes sense to learn more about these adversaries that reside in your own skull. You can increase your ability to maintain your "write mind" (the mind that supports a regular and productive writing practice) by paying attention to what is happening in there.

I encourage writers to identify their personal versions of the terrifying visions that create disabling emotions about their work. What apparitions arise in your mind that generate feelings such as fear, dread, powerlessness, anger, confusion, and overwhelm? A doctoral student in his eighth year of work on his dissertation was incapacitated by intrusive memories of the misdeeds of his hostile and sadistic faculty advisor. A screenwriter was afraid to write rough drafts because of fantasies that he would unexpectedly die and someone would find his unpolished pages and conclude that he was a bad writer. An aspiring fiction writer would consistently hear a loud internal voice telling her she had no right to pretend to be a writer. There are infinite variations of such stories that have the same underlying dynamic: thoughts, memories, and fantasies arise in our imagination and generate disturbing emotions that then interfere with writing. Here are some thoughts about thoughts that might help you remain in your write mind.

⊙ *Thoughts that contribute to writing blocks are almost always automatically repeating habits of thinking.*

Most of the thoughts that disrupt your writing are not mysterious or new. These patterns were established in your younger, formative years and carried forward into adulthood. You can identify them by placing a bit of attention on your inner mental and emotional processes. The bad news is that these repeating, well-grooved patterns of thinking occur quickly and powerfully, often before your conscious mind knows what has happened. You might be aware of what they are; you might not.

The good news is that, because you are equipped with a magnificent human brain, you can learn to identify these patterns and consciously decrease their debilitating impact on your writing productivity. It is not too hard to pick out the thought patterns once you concentrate on this task, because they occur over and over. Some people can identify particular internal voices that spout criticism, insults, or prophecies of doom. More than one of my students has even had a name and visual image of their "inner harasser."

Identifying debilitating patterns of thought

⊙ *Harmful thoughts can occur without your noticing or questioning them.*

The mental activities that accompany blocks typically occur without your conscious choice and even possibly without your awareness. You may experience uncomfortable feelings about writing but fail to notice the dark inner dialogues and fantasies behind the scenes that are wreaking havoc. In these inner dialogues you might be saying something terribly frightening or critical about yourself or the project. It is equally possible to be aware of disturbing physical sensations connected to writing without having a clear idea of why you are experiencing them. Or you may simply notice that you are repeatedly unable to bring yourself to your desk, without knowing why. Feelings of powerlessness and frustration are intensified when there is a lack of understanding about the inner dynamics that are dictating your self-sabotaging behavior. This confusion sets the scene for a depressing spiral of apprehension, decreased confidence, and increased aversion to writing.

Bring Your Writing Back to Life!

⊙ *Your thoughts generate emotional and behavioral responses that influence your writing productivity.*

It is a cruel irony that your own thoughts create the very feelings that give you a sense of being hampered or victimized. When you experience anxiety, anger, overwhelm, or dread about writing it is because you have generated these feelings. It might seem strange to look at your emotional life this way, but give it a try. It is tempting to believe you have no choice about the feelings you experience, but this is only partially true. There are some things you can do to change the quality and intensity of your inner experience.

     A woman in one of my classes spoke about how much she *hated* writing. She also wanted desperately to write because she *loved* to write. This predicament is not uncommon. It feels agonizing to do it and impossible to give it up. I asked her if it was *writing* she hated, or the *disturbing feelings* that arise when she writes. This difference is not trivial. If you realize that the emotions that interfere with your productivity are unfortunate mental habits that you are perpetuating, you then have the opportunity to try to change them. Below are two perspectives that can help you in this regard.

⊙ *Just because we think or feel something, that doesn't make it true.*

Debilitating thoughts that plague writers (e.g., "I have no talent," "I will fail if I attempt this," or "I am not a writer") are generally exaggerations and distortions of the truth that have gained too much authority and power due to their endless internal repetition. It is a form of self-inflicted brainwashing in which the struggling writer is both the terrorist and the terrorized. Dragging these thoughts into the clear light of day and examining them more objectively is one method of freeing yourself from being bullied and controlled by them. They are mental habits we have learned, not immutable "Truths." They are also temporary experiences. Sometimes all we have to do is wait them out and they will go away.

● *If you become more aware of the mental processes connected with your blocks, you will at least have a fighting chance of escaping their control.*

Pay attention to emotions and body sensations

There are some things you can do to alter your inner experience. Start by identifying your own particular set of thoughts and feelings about writing. The self-assessments presented earlier should help with this. If nothing seems to emerge for you in the form of an identifiable thought, pay attention to emotions and body sensations connected with your writing. These are usually recurrent patterns as well, and sometimes with a bit of effort and focus you can identify the thoughts connected with emotions and sensations. The most common problematic thoughts generate the emotions of fear, resentment, hopelessness, or overwhelm. Look for these. If you are only aware of feeling blank or daydreaming, try to notice subtle or faint feelings that may provide clues about what you are saying to yourself.

Bring Your Writing Back to Life!

Mental and Emotional Perspectives Associated with Writing Problems

In order to identify as specifically as possible the demons that put you out of your write mind, try to hear the thoughts as if they were spoken in the form of a sentence. This makes them concrete and easier to contend with. Here are some examples that might prime the pump.

All or nothing	"If the best journal doesn't accept my article, it's been a waste of time writing it."
Arrogance	"I'm a very talented writer and I don't have to prove it by writing something."
Boredom	"I'd like to write more but it's such drudgery."
Catastrophic thinking	"If I don't write this paper, I'll fail the class and flunk out of school. Then I won't be able to get a job and I'll end up living on the street."
Critical of one's own work	"My story is crap."
Denial	"This time the project should flow smoothly."
Difficulties with decisions	"I'll leave it in. Nope, I'll take it out. Nah, I better keep it in. But it looks out of place there."
Dread	"The process of writing this paper is going to be horrific!"
Dread of criticism	"I will wither and die if she tells me she doesn't like my poem."
Discounting	"Yes, several publishers told me they wanted to publish the book, but that doesn't mean it's any good."

Exaggerate difficulties	"This memo is going to take an enormous amount of time and effort to complete."
Fear of loss of control	"What is wrong with me? I can't seem to make myself write. Am I losing it? Do I have early-onset Alzheimer's?"
Forgetfulness	"Oops! I forgot to write during the last decade."
Guilt	"I'm disappointing others because of my writing problems."
Grandiosity	"My novel will be the next *Moby Dick*."
Haunted by the past	"This is going to be a nightmare, just like the last article."
Hopelessness	"Why should I bother? It will just be another miserable failure."
Impatience	"I am writing too slowly. This is taking way too long."
Imposter feelings	"When they read this crap they will find out I'm not a real writer."
Indolence	"I just don't feel like writing right now. It'll be OK to do it later."
Judgmental	"His article is absolute junk. I couldn't live with myself if I wrote like that."
Low self-esteem	"I am a worthless person because of my writing problems."
Overwhelm	"There is so much to do I don't know where to begin! I'll never be able to do it all!"

Bring Your Writing Back to Life!

Minimize capabilities	"I don't have enough energy to work on that project." "I can write an article, but there is no way I could write a book."
Panic	"Oh my God! I can't breathe! Heart attack! I'm going crazy!"
Perfectionism	"Every word in this first draft needs to be perfect."
Pessimism	"There is no way they will publish my article."
Rationalizing	"Well, I would have had an 'A' if I had spent more time on it."
Rebelliousness	"If I don't feel like writing, you can't make me."
Resentment	"I hate writing."
Self-criticism	"I'm a lousy writer."
Self-limiting beliefs	"I can write only when I feel inspired." "I can write only when there is a gun pointed at my head." "I can write only when I have many hours of free time." "I can't start writing until I've got the whole novel figured out."
Should and shouldn't	"I should be writing more. I should be writing better. I should be able to write without so much struggle. I shouldn't feel so anxious about writing."
Specialness	"My writing is a very special part of me and I don't want to risk losing that by exposing my work to criticism from the public."
Superstitions	"If I finish my book I will die."

THE BLOCKED WRITER'S BOOK OF THE DEAD

Time-estimation errors   "I'll have plenty of time later to write this article."

"This article will take forever to do. I can't face it."

Uncertainty   "I don't know how to write this next chapter."

Unrealistic standards   "My novel has to be as good as *Moby Dick*."

Other thoughts:

_____
_____
_____
_____

Bring Your Writing Back to Life!

⊙ *You also have access to helpful and adaptive ways of thinking.*

You may or may not be aware that you also have supportive, encouraging, and empowering patterns of thinking that can and do help you write. Refer back to the exercise in Chapter 5 where you listed your abilities and talents with writing. Consciously accessing and highlighting these thoughts and beliefs is an approach that has helped some writers. Use memories of past successes, validations from others, inspirations, and feelings of competence or pleasure that have been connected to your writing. Bring these thoughts into your mind when you notice the negative patterns asserting themselves, to counter the negativity and reconnect with your strengths.

Generate a short list of the dominant thoughts about writing that populate your mental universe, and notice how frequently they pop up in your mind during the day. With practice you will get better at this. When you notice you are procrastinating, for instance, shift your attention to what you are feeling and thinking. Catch your mental processes in the act, without judging yourself, and study them. Be curious about your amazing mind. Can you pinpoint the inner voices most responsible for your difficulties? Are you able to see how these voices might be exaggerated, inaccurate, or distorted? How do these thoughts sound if you say them out loud, or to another person? Which thoughts assist you in maintaining consistent writing, or returning to writing? The goal is to develop the ability to recognize thoughts as just being thoughts, and feelings as being nothing more than feelings. Watch them come into your awareness and let them float away. Then get back to writing.

Chapter 11

Feelings

"And again, at that time, thou wilt be feeling very miserable. Be not miserable in that way."

~ *The Tibetan Book of the Dead*

If you increase your capacity to accept, feel, tolerate, and understand the emotional side of your nature, you will increase your capacity to write. Writing is much more than an intellectual pursuit, and emotions are inextricably woven into the process, in both obvious and subtle ways. You *feel* something when you anticipate writing. You *feel* something while you write. Then you *feel* something when you read what you have written, or when someone else does. Some feelings help writing productivity, some don't. Emotions provide the necessary fuel to motivate you to pick up the pen in spite of the effort and struggle involved. Emotions help you evaluate when something you've written *feels* right or wrong. Emotions can also be difficult internal experiences to battle with, flee from, cling to, or ignore.

One of the problems with emotions is that they are powerful and they operate much faster than your conscious mind does. It is not always easy to see what is happening in the moments when you are deciding whether you will write or not, and your conditioned emotional responses often determine the outcome.

Bring Your Writing Back to Life!

Every writer I have ever met experiences emotional discomfort occasionally or frequently while writing or thinking about writing. Even if you don't fully understand where your difficult feelings come from, you can learn to increase your tolerance for these internal states and in so doing, gain greater control of your writing.

Allow yourself to feel emotions such as fear, resentment, shame, inadequacy, and ambivalence, without automatically responding with attempts to repress or flee from their intensity. They're just feelings. You are going to survive. You will grow stronger by allowing your body to go through emotionally intense states without panicking. These are time-limited experiences. Some part of you may feel like you will certainly die if you sit down to write, but you won't. Take baby steps in this direction and see what happens. Do just a little bit more writing when disturbing feelings arrive, instead of moving away from your project. No need to be heroic. You are building up your writing muscles bit by bit. These small changes have big consequences if you keep it up.

One method of reducing emotional discomfort when you want to write is to practice relaxing. Distressing feelings are almost always connected with muscular tension, and if you gain some control over the tension, the feelings will have less power over your decisions about writing. I recommend taking three minutes to relax when you start to write or when you are stuck. Sit quietly in a comfortable chair, close your eyes, and take three deep breaths. Then tune into the muscles in your face, tongue, jaws, and hands. Just pay attention to how these muscles feel, and let go of any tightness you notice there. When your notice your mind has wandered, bring your attention back to these muscles and see if you can relax them more. This tends to quiet the mind. Don't be discouraged if you don't get immediate relief: the more you practice this technique, the more effective it will become.

Reducing emotional discomfort

91

Quite a few writers I know find it useful to do something physical, like pacing or hiking, when they are engaged in a writing project. Sometimes a repetitive physical activity engages the mind in a helpful way that allows the writing mind to function better. Any exercise that promotes blood flow in the body, and especially in the brain, is helpful.

Another method of handling uncomfortable or distressing thoughts and feelings during a writing session is to pause and write them down when they arrive. Tell yourself you will consider these issues when your writing session is done, and return to your project.

Chapter 12

The Judgment

"... do not speak against me concerning what I have done, do not bring up anything against me in the presence of the Great God..."
~ *The Egyptian Book of the Dead*

"... thou needst not be afraid. The Lords of Death are thine own hallucinations."
~ *The Tibetan Book of the Dead*

With surprising similarity both *The Egyptian Book of the Dead* and *The Tibetan Book of the Dead* describe a pivotal sequence in the afterlife called "The Judgment," during which the deceased's character and deeds on Earth are reviewed and evaluated. The gods Thoth (Egyptian) and Yama, Lord of Death (Tibetan), conduct ruthlessly thorough post-mortem examinations of each soul's earthly deeds, and those unfortunates with an excess of black marks on their ledger are sentenced to either additional rounds of suffering on Earth or to a more enduring damnation in agonizing hells or lakes of fire. Needless to say, it is very important to make it through this crucial juncture successfully, and both books of the dead offer considerable coaching on this point.

Writers don't have to wait until they die to meet the Lord of Death—they experience The Judgment every day. These judgments come from teachers, professors, parents, editors, friends, classmates, colleagues, the public, reviewers, and significant others. Writing is a social enterprise, and if your writing becomes public in any way,

Acid-tongued internal critics

there will be judgments to contend with. As previously discussed, real or imagined negative evaluations from others can inhibit you from writing at all.

In addition, the inner lords of death, self-judgments, can be particularly damning, and also damming, to the flow of writing. As writers, we frequently endure the caustic heckling of these acid-tongued internal critics. It comes with the territory. Obviously, it's not so easy to get into an enthusiastic, productive writing groove if the soundtrack of your writing life is a corrosive tirade of criticism and self-loathing. In severe cases, each and every word put to paper comes under an unforgiving and time-consuming laser-like scrutiny of evaluation and condemnation. There is a place for a perfectionist's eye in the writing process, but if it runs amok too early on, your inspirations will be snuffed out before they have a chance to unfold and mature. And your writing becomes as much fun as a swim in the lake of fire.

If you secretly cherish a stratospherically high evaluation of your talents, you may also run the risk of not writing because the acid test of putting your work out into the world is a potential threat to your attractive self-view. Your ego senses the danger that comes with receiving feedback. The reading public might not share your opinion, and this could deflate the appealing self-image you have constructed.

Even well-deserved, positive evaluations of your writing can lead to blocks. A young woman in a writing group had an impressive reception to work she published in her early twenties and then she locked up for years. Like Wily Coyote when he runs off a cliff chasing the Roadrunner, she did great until she looked down and realized how high above the ground she was. There is so far to fall when you're up that high. Her success exceeded her self-confidence by too great a margin, and she was plagued by the conviction that it was a fluke and she would not be able to do it again, yet she also felt it would be a terrible failure if she didn't.

Bring Your Writing Back to Life!

It is often, if not always, true that the impact of others' opinions affect us most when they mirror beliefs or fears we carry within us. Everyone has a style of dealing with real or anticipated feedback. What is yours?

Here are some questions to help you consider this issue.

Do you carry an internal image of the audience you are writing for when you write?
_____

Does this "imagined audience" help or hinder your progress and productivity?
_____

How?
_____
_____
_____

Do you avoid showing your work to others due to fears about how they will react?
_____

Do you feel like an imposter who will be discovered if others read your work?
_____

Do you imagine scenes where people important to you are reacting to your writing?
_____

THE BLOCKED WRITER'S BOOK OF THE DEAD

How are these fantasies helpful or harmful to your writing process?

What are your real or imagined "worst case scenarios" regarding criticism and rejection?

How have specific incidents of criticism affected your productivity?

How have specific incidents of praise affected your productivity?

Can you identify the people in your life who have helped or harmed you with their feedback? Who were they and what did they do?

What is the difference between the type of feedback that has helped your productivity and feedback that resulted in blocks?

Bring Your Writing Back to Life!

How critical are you of other people's writing? If you are quite critical of others, do you apply the same harsh criticism to your own work?

_____
_____
_____

Real or imagined judgments might inhibit you as a writer, but you can develop strategies that mitigate the impact of these issues. Here are some examples of how to do that.

- **Know your sensitivities and respect them—to a point. Gradually increase your tolerance for receiving feedback to your work.**

If you are quite sensitive and avoidant about showing your work to others, but would like to be able to, start carefully and thoughtfully. View this as an ability you will cultivate over time in a step-by-step way. Be patient and avoid comparing yourself to people who do not seem to have the same struggles. It doesn't matter what other people feel or do. Our social and interpersonal habits are typically long-standing and resilient patterns that are connected with many different, powerful feelings. Change in this area is possible but should be approached wisely and gradually. Even minor changes that involve being more social or public about your writing are significant victories. Each step strengthens your hide, teaches you something about yourself and others, and lays the groundwork for going further. A supportive class or workshop is sometimes a good way to start becoming more public with your writing.

No writer escapes negative feedback

⊙ *Choose the right time to ask for feedback.*

Your writing project will go through many stages on the way to completion. There are numerous points along the way when you might benefit from input, and other times when you should keep your writing private. Everyone is different in terms of what works best. Common stages in a writing project include:

- generating ideas

- doing research

- organizing notes

- making an outline

- writing a first draft

- refining and revising additional drafts

- final editing

- submitting the completed work

- revisions and resubmission (if needed)

- beginning a new project

Bring Your Writing Back to Life!

⊙ *Consider your work style and identify where in this process you are most likely to have problems.*

During which phase(s) are you most at risk to procrastinate or block?

_____

During which phase(s) would you benefit the most from input?

_____

Some writers do not like to have their ideas or stories made public too early in the process, out of concern that the project needs to gestate internally longer to develop properly, without interference. Others like a lot of interaction in the beginning stages to help them brainstorm and focus on what they really want to write about. Identify your preferred stages and consider how feedback might be of use to you at that time. Experiment with involving people at different phases of your projects and go with what feels right.

⊙ *Choose the right people to show your work to.*

Some people in your life will help you become more productive—and some will not. It is essential to recognize the difference. Some readers have the ability to give feedback that is thoughtful, sensitive, useful, and honest. Some will give glowing praise about everything you show them. Others, intentionally or not, will stomp your ego flat because of ignorance, insensitivity, or their own unresolved issues with their own writing. If you have a history of being terrified or even just apprehensive about the process of showing your work and receiving feedback, avoid these types. You certainly don't need any additional bad experiences related to this issue.

Start off by selecting a reader or listener you trust. Someone who is unlikely to assault your self-esteem, such as a pet cat. When you are ready to approach a human reader, choose someone who is at least somewhat kind, and then ask him or her to read your work without giving you any sort of feedback about it. This affords you some safety in order to take the first step of coming out of the closet with less risk. As you gain comfort with doing this, you can begin asking for reactions, perhaps initially requesting to hear only what the reader liked about the piece. At this beginning stage, if the person you chose cannot do this, and feels compelled to "help" you by pointing out flaws and suggesting "improvements," then find someone else. There will be time for constructive criticism later, after your tolerance for handling feedback has grown stronger.

Your best writing advisors may not be the people you are closest to. This is unfortunate but frequently true. Significant others, family members, and best friends are obvious choices for readers, but their close relationship with you may make them unable to give you useful and objective feedback, no matter how much you love them. This can be especially true when your significant other is also a writer. It's OK to keep your work private if that is the case, and to help your loved ones understand why you need that. If it works to include them at some phase of the process—great!

◉ *Specify the type of feedback you are seeking, and the feedback you don't want.*

Not only does this help you, it helps your reader as well. If you need input on a character you are creating and instead get a lot of feedback about punctuation, it will be irritating. If you are in the initial stages of a project and want reactions to the general concept and structure of the piece, tell your reader to focus on that and to ignore imperfections in the sentences and grammar. This gives you a certain amount of control over how much emotional stress you will experience, and better odds of getting the responses you need to help move your project along.

⊙ *Rehearse worst case scenarios and develop plans for survival.*

Whether you are anticipating feedback from your grandmother, a teacher, or the editor of the premier journal in your field, there is always a chance that something you hear from that person could traumatize you. It is useful to mentally consider the worst case situation and imagine how you will successfully cope with that. Remind yourself that you will survive, and that you can disregard the criticism that comes from ignorance or is gratuitously hostile and mean-spirited, and use the constructive criticism to improve your work. Imagine yourself continuing to write successfully even if the worst case were to occur. Know whom you can talk to for perspective, support, and encouragement. Remember, no piece of writing will please everyone; even Shakespeare has his detractors. The important thing about mental preparation is that it can decrease the chances that negative feedback will *prevent you from writing*. Negative feedback is a powerful block generator and no writer escapes this challenge completely, no matter what successes he or she has experienced.

⊙ *Have revision and resubmission plans.*

When awaiting a response to a submission to a publisher or literary agent, it is empowering to have backup plans for how you will continue to promote your manuscript in the event of a rejection. There is a good chance your submission will be going to an editor you don't know, where it will be considered in a selection process whose outcome is determined by numerous variables and influences you have no control over. Don't let this process affect your willingness to continue writing. Keep in mind that *The Cat in the Hat* was rejected by 50 publishers before it was accepted. Revise and resubmit if possible, or find another place to submit your work. Over time you will develop the skill of not taking the rejections so personally that they prevent you from writing the next day.

◉ *Keep more than one project going.*

If you are waiting to hear about the acceptance or rejection of a piece, it can be a psychological buffer to know you have another project in the pipeline. You are not putting all your eggs in one unpredictable basket. By working on something new, you also decrease your anxiety by bringing your mental energy to a productive focus rather than obsessing about someone else's opinion or decision about your work. Plus, you are creating another piece that might bear fruit if the one before it doesn't, and you are continuing to strengthen your routine of regular writing.

◉ *Continue writing after a project is completed.*

It is natural to want to take a break when you have completed a project, especially one that has been challenging and lengthy. This gap time between projects is, however, a high-risk juncture for initiating an extended period of work avoidance. If you take a break of a few days, have a plan in place about when you will begin writing again. It should be more specific than "I'll get going in a while, when I feel rested and inspired again." Pick a date and time in the near future that you will set aside to return to your writing schedule, even if it is only for a few minutes a day. Keep at least one toe in the water.

Bring Your Writing Back to Life!

⊙ *"What will help the writing?"*

None of us can completely separate our feelings about our "self" when judgments are made about our writing. But perhaps we can move in that direction just enough to prevent criticism and rejection from paralyzing our writing muscles. One way to do this is to keep asking, "What will help the writing?" You will benefit more if your mind is focused on that question rather than on whether or not you are an imposter or an idiot or stupid or worthless or boring or magnificent. After all, our lives are a mystery—we don't really know what is going on, and all the time we spend protecting, defending, rationalizing, loathing, and lauding our sense of self is, at the end of the day, a pointless exercise in generating pain. Maybe it would be better to spend what precious little time we have on the planet doing *anything else* instead of that. Of course, this is easier said than done, but you can always direct at least some tiny bit of effort toward doing something else. Something that will leave you with a sense of accomplishment and satisfaction. Something that has the potential to make a contribution. Something like writing.

Taking in feedback without wilting

By keeping your primary focus on how to make your writing better, rather than on how criticism and rejection make you feel, you also cultivate a degree of openness and tolerance for receiving important feedback that is not complimentary. It is essential for your growth and development as a writer to be able to take in such information without wilting completely. The perceptive minds of others offer a storehouse of information, and you can benefit from knowing what they think is good, or not so good, about your work. Even some nasty, ill-tempered remarks will potentially be useful to you if they contain a grain of truth. You will be more willing and less threatened to hear tough but true words about your work if you believe those words will help you write better. Even if they come from the mouth of a jerk.

As noted in the passage from *The Tibetan Book of the Dead* at the start of this chapter, the fears and resentments we experience in the process of placing our pages in front of the public are our own. These feelings can be triggered by imagined feedback or by our actual interactions with others, but they are our own feelings, and they can stop the writing. The bad news is that we habitually feed and reinforce these inner demons that control us. The good news is that like many demons, their bark is worse than their actual bite. The best news is that we can learn to tame them, a little bit at a time.

Chapter 13

Encountering the Unknown

"Thick, awesome darkness will appear in front of thee continually."
~ *The Tibetan Book of the Dead*

Writing, like dying, involves an unavoidable confrontation with the unknown. We don't know exactly what will happen when we sit down to write. In the gap between initiating and completing a writing project, we have many opportunities to observe how we deal with the unknown.

The unknown might be a sentence not yet right, a mountain of information not yet organized, an argument not yet developed, a problem not yet solved, or a story line not yet worked out. We know something more needs to be accomplished, and we don't know exactly how we will do it. This moment of contemplating the unknown is fertile territory for spawning anxiety, self-doubt, confidence crises, and work avoidance. The experience of not knowing may also make a person feel that something internal is lacking: intelligence, creativity, or other unnamable attributes that "real" writers supposedly possess.

What is your characteristic mode of responding when you don't know how to proceed? During the writing of my dissertation

I repeatedly confronted new problems and challenges I had no ready solutions for. In my mind, each one of these problems was a dark torpedo screaming toward my dissertation's brittle hull. I would back away from the project with each challenge because my catastrophic fantasizing made the writing hard to tolerate. Eventually I'd return to my desk and the problems would somehow be resolved after I wrestled with them for a while. The ship stayed afloat and I eventually learned to settle down and trust the process.

Here are some of the responses that the encounter with the unknown evokes in writers I have worked with. Do any of these sound familiar to you?

___ Not beginning a project due to uncertainty of how to begin or thinking that all problems need to be resolved before starting to write.

___ Feeling overwhelmed when contemplating the organizational challenges of a project.

___ Losing confidence that you will be able to do what is required, then avoiding work to reduce discomfort.

___ Feeling fraudulent for not having answers to problems that "real" writers would have no trouble with.

___ Being impatient with the pace of the process of resolving the project's challenges.

___ Becoming obsessed with the passing of time while feeling stuck and not producing.

___ Decreased ability to concentrate and write effectively due to anxiety generated by contemplating unresolved problems.

___ Interpreting the unavoidable reflective pauses that occur during writing as "blocks" and worrying that the pauses are evidence of incompetence or proof that the project is not going to come out right.

___ Retreating into extensive reading binges to fill in presumed gaps of knowledge.

___ Working excessively long hours to gain a sense of control but having little to show for it.

___ Experiencing feelings of shame or humiliation while anticipating failure, and then procrastinating to avoid those feelings.

As you can see from the list above, several of the issues connected with facing the unknown are linked to procrastination. Can you imagine making friends with the "thick, awesome darkness" when it appears? One strategy is to consciously cultivate a greater degree of acceptance and tolerance for the uncertainties of the writing process. Remind yourself that these moments are an unavoidable and necessary part of creating something new. Be patient when things aren't immediately clear. If you are in the process of clarifying something or doing a task for the first time, things may proceed gradually, especially with projects that are covering new ground or that are complex.

"Unknown" doesn't have to mean terrifying, daunting, or painful. In fact, for many writers it is the appeal of creating something that doesn't yet exist in the world that propels them to write. The encounter with the unknown is where the thrills and gratification lie, as well as the hardships. It is where interesting things happen.

Be curious when you feel stumped. Pause and ponder the problem, and see if you can witness your emotional responses in a more dispassionate way. As discussed in Chapter 10, **Not in Your Write Mind**, try to hang out in the uncertainty without panicking or bolting. The writing issue you are trying to resolve may indeed be a challenging one, but it's your emotional reactions that turn a challenge into a block. Try not to abandon your efforts too quickly. Stay in there for a while and notice what happens. See if you can calm yourself by taking a few deep breaths and relaxing the muscles of your face, jaw, neck, shoulders, and arms. If it is just a wave of emotion, maybe you can ride it out and keep going. Take a deep breath.

Shifting to freewriting

Another tactic is to switch to freewriting for five or ten minutes and see what bubbles up from that process. Freewriting, as described in Peter Elbow's book *Writing Without Teachers,* is simply writing any and all words that come to mind without pausing and without trying to censor or control what comes out. The freewriting itself may yield new ideas or clues to a helpful approach, and it is also useful as a recuperative shift of focus for your stressed-out mind while deeper processes work on the solutions.

You might also benefit from conversations with other people when you feel bewildered. The process of talking about your predicament in conversation often results in a productive shift. (Those of us in the therapy business are very grateful that things work this way.) It's not necessary to find a listener who will solve the problem for you, just one who is able to lend a sympathetic and thoughtful ear while you discover your own answers. If you don't generally talk with others about writing or ask anyone for help, it may initially feel uncomfortable to do so. I have found that blocked writers are often too isolated and private about their work, and if they begin to take even modest steps to involve other people in their writing process, good things begin to happen.

You may encounter the unknown because you actually need to know more about your topic before you can proceed. Doing additional research may feel like a hassle that will be too time consuming, but in the long run more time will be wasted in trying to proceed without having necessary information. But look out for getting lost on the Web or in the library researching issues that are only slightly relevant, because that feels more comfortable than writing.

"But," you might ask, "what if I feel like I am beating a dead horse?" If you are in a lengthy struggle to resolve a writing problem and your efforts are only making you more anxious, frustrated, and exhausted, it may be wise to shift gears and do something else for a while. Move to a different, less challenging part of the project, work on another project, or do something unrelated to writing. Sometimes answers come into focus if you take a break and chew on the issues subconsciously. If you do take a break from writing to let your dead horse catch its breath, make it a conscious decision and have a plan for returning to the writing.

Hitting an impasse may also mean that you are too exhausted, hungry, or stressed out to think clearly and work effectively. A writer can easily forget about the body. Sleep, exercise, and food are essential to keep the writing machine operational. An aspiring novelist, who was also a store manager and the father of four children, decided that the only free time he had to write was from four to six in the morning. The trouble was that he never went to bed before midnight. His plan to write from four to six lasted two days. Respect your indispensable ally, your body, and notice when your fuel gauge is on "E."

Exhaustion, hunger, and stress

Chapter 14

Rebirth: Improving Writing Productivity

Below is a set of tips and recommendations for improving your writing productivity; these ideas and suggestions address many different aspects of the writing process. By now you probably have a sense of which areas need the most attention to improve your productivity as a writer. Check the items below that will contribute most to your writing efforts.

Time

___ Create a routine time for writing (daily is best).

___ Schedule an optimal daily amount. Short, regular sessions of less than an hour are recommended following a non-productive period.

___ Protect your writing time.

___ Be realistic in planning projects and setting expectations. Start with small, realizable goals.

___ Maintain a balance between writing and other responsibilities and activities in your life.

Bring Your Writing Back to Life!

___ Maintain a consistent daily output when working with long-term deadlines.

___ Keep in mind that binge writing at deadline maintains patterns of blocking.

Space

___ Have a place to write that is comfortable, easy to get to, and functional.

___ Arrange your space to minimize exposure to your highest risk distractions (cookie jars, telephones, televisions, etc.).

___ Do not begin a writing session by cleaning and organizing your work space; do this after you have written.

Getting Started

___ Have your writing place stocked with necessary materials.

___ Recall times in the past when you wrote productively. What were your patterns of writing then? What can you apply from those times to your present situation?

___ Establish or re-establish a consistent habit and ritual of daily writing.

___ If you are just staring at the monitor or page and are having difficulty getting started, try warming up with a brief period of freewriting. This could be five or ten minutes of writing down anything that comes to mind without concern about the nature or quality of the content.

Changing Behavior

___ Make a chart of your daily writing productivity. Put it on the refrigerator.

___ Analyze each writing project and break it into bite-sized chunks.

___ Make success unavoidable each day by having goals that would be hard not to attain.

___ Start with modest expectations, especially after a non-productive period.

___ Make a list of your most common work-avoiding behaviors (e.g., eating, taking a bath, e-mailing, TV watching, non-essential busywork, etc.). Develop strategies for reducing the likelihood of engaging in each of those activities during writing time.

___ Notice if you are reinforcing the pattern of avoiding writing. Do you reward yourself when you do not write by engaging in pleasure-seeking activities during writing time?

___ If needed, make a desired daily activity contingent upon having done some writing. This might mean denying yourself exercise, reading the newspaper, talking on the phone, playing piano, watching a favorite show, or taking a shower unless a minimum amount of writing has occurred.

Bring Your Writing Back to Life!

Thoughts and Feelings

___ Notice your "self-talk" about writing. Pay particular attention to those thoughts that are frightening, critical, demoralizing, and overwhelming. These thoughts generate distressing feelings that may interfere with our writing productivity.

___ When you notice negative thoughts invading, consciously replace unhelpful messages with positive, hopeful thoughts; reminding yourself of previous successes and the abilities you possess. This process becomes more effective with practice.

___ Be mindful of patterns of placing perfectionistic, unrealistic, or excessively rigid demands on your writing process or content. An unreasonably harsh internal critic is a common feature among blocked writers. Practice with freewriting can help temper these.

___ If anxiety or depression becomes chronic or intense, seek professional assistance.

People Issues

___ Develop and utilize relationships with colleagues or other writers you can share your work with.

___ Be specific about the kind of feedback you want or do not want when sharing your work with others.

___ Work collaboratively with another writer(s) on a project.

___ Avoid isolation: maintain or rekindle professional and personal contacts, especially if blocking is a problem.

___ Determine if there are any unresolved interpersonal issues with significant people (colleague, mentor, dissertation advisor, boss, spouse) that may be affecting your writing. Make efforts to address these problems.

___ If you have difficulty showing your writing to others, begin with people you like and trust, and who are unlikely to savage your work. Slowly branch out from there to include others. A group or class often provides a supportive environment for going public with your writing.

Chapter 15

Your Writing Productivity Improvement Plan

This is a section for creating your own writing productivity plan. Take a few minutes to fill out this section, even if you feel some resistance to doing so, and use the items from the tips in the previous chapter as an aid. Making a plan is an act of commitment to yourself and your writing that will increase the odds that you will put what you have learned from this book into practice.

The process of creating your **Writing Productivity Improvement Plan** involves remembering and honoring your desire to write, deciding what writing project is most important to start with, knowing your strengths and challenges, selecting realistic and appropriate steps to take, and developing strategies for reconnecting to writing if you fall off the wagon. You may want to keep a copy of this plan in a conspicuous place to remind yourself of your commitment. It may also help to let someone else know you have made a plan about your writing. Just imagining that a friend might ask you about your progress could motivate you to stay on track.

If you find yourself anxious, overwhelmed, or highly resistant to taking this step of committing to a plan, consider filling out just one section of it per day over the next week. On the seventh day you can rest and review what you've accomplished and see that it is good. There is no rush; the important thing is that you are continuing to move a step forward every day—even if the steps appear small. No step is a small step if you've been blocked.

Bring Your Writing Back to Life!

Writing Productivity Improvement Plan

1. In a single sentence, explain why it is important for you to write regularly (refer to the **Motivations for Writing** checklist on page 45).

    _____
    _____
    _____

2. What writing project(s) would you most like to make progress on?

    _____
    _____
    _____

Do you have externally dictated deadlines? If not, create a realistic time frame for completing it (them).

    _____
    _____
    _____

3. Recall a time when you wrote relatively well on a project (refer to the **Writing Assets, Strengths, and Abilities** checklist on page 39).

    _____
    _____
    _____

What abilities, talents, habits, and personal qualities contributed to your success?

    _____
    _____
    _____

THE BLOCKED WRITER'S BOOK OF THE DEAD

How did you schedule writing time, and where did you write?

What was your mood and state of mind like?

Did anyone else contribute to making that a positive experience? How?

Are there elements of that experience that could be applied to your current projects?

4. List the primary challenges to your writing productivity (refer to the **Self-Assessment** on page 28).

   a. _____

   b. _____

   c. _____

Bring Your Writing Back to Life!

5. For each challenge identified, generate one idea (select from the **Improving Productivity** list in the previous chapter or create your own) for addressing some aspect of the problem that you can take action on *in the next week*. Post a copy of this "Set of Solutions" where you write, on your refrigerator, and anywhere else it might be helpful to have it. Make a check mark on it and note the date each time you implement a planned solution.

   a. _____

   b. _____

   c. _____

6. Generate one idea (select from the **Improving Productivity** tips in the previous chapter or create your own) for addressing three of your primary challenges that you can take action on *in the next month*. Update and amend as needed. Post a copy of this **Set of Solutions** where you write, on your refrigerator, and anywhere else it might be helpful to have it. Make a check mark on it and note the date each time you implement a planned solution.

   a. _____

   b. _____

   c. _____

7. Congratulate yourself for valuing yourself as a writer, for deciding to consciously address your writing habits, and for having the courage and willingness to spend the time and effort required to improve them.

Dealing with Relapses

If you find that you are unable to make a plan, or that you start off well but get blocked again after a while, do not despair. This is not a sign that there is no hope, only that there are additional issues that need to be addressed. Such difficulties are more the norm than the exception. There may be a few or several false starts along the way to establishing your connection with regular writing, and you may find there is always a gap between your goals and your performance. This is normal, and you don't have to hate yourself or give up hope because of it.

When you recognize that you are not writing, there are several things you can do that will help.

1. Find your **Writing Productivity Improvement Plan**. Pick one action item and do it. It should be something simple and brief.

2. Write for five minutes, then stop. Do this every day for a week and see what happens. If you can't write on your project yet, write about anything, without judging the content.

3. Don't get too isolated. Contact someone you trust who is a good listener, and discuss your dilemma.

4. Amend your writing plan if needed. Initial steps should move you forward but not be too challenging to complete.

5. Offer support and encouragement to someone else who is struggling with writing. Helping others can serve your writing as well.

6. Remind yourself of why you want to write. Review your **Motivations for Writing** checklist on page 45.

7. Remind yourself of your writing strengths. Review your **Writing Assets, Talents, and Abilities** checklist on page 39.

The goal is to try to reengage with the writing process and to start writing consistently again. A little bit of writing each day is a powerful way to break the cycle of avoidance, and it sets the stage for you to enjoy and feel confident about writing again. You may find you have to confront your demons and work with your mind, emotions, and relationships before you can write for even five minutes. Every writer has to find the approach that works for him or her. The greatest predictor of success will be your willingness to keep at it; to return to writing, even when the resistance is powerful.

Final Thoughts

As a writer, you are on a journey. From your early youth you have been expressing yourself using the written word, and you have developed an interest and a passion for writing. In your journey as a writer you have encountered numerous challenges; some coming from the outside world and some generated by your own mind. At times these challenges may have slowed down the flow of the words and ideas you desired to express, or perhaps stopped them dead.

The Tibetan Book of the Dead and *The Egyptian Book of the Dead* are roadmaps for attaining salvation. They offer guidance, warning, encouragement, and wisdom for souls embarking on the challenging journey to the worlds beyond this one. Both books stress the importance of maintaining an awareness of one's vulnerability and the importance of respecting the powerful and mysterious forces that control our lives. It is also implicit in both books that you can improve your fate by understanding yourself, paying attention to the situations you encounter, and working skillfully with the challenges that arise. The desired result is a transformation of the meaning of death from a depressing annihilation into an opportunity to attain a joyful and blessed eternity. *The Blocked Writer's Book of the Dead* has a similar goal: the transformation of depressing blocks and procrastination into a joyful and blessed flow of words.

I hope that by reading this book you have developed a deeper understanding of your writing process, and have identified at least a few ideas or suggestions that will assist you or inspire you to bring your writing back to life. I also hope you have developed a greater sense of appreciation and compassion for yourself as you experience the wonderful rewards and awesome challenges of producing the written word.

Appendix

The Puppy Principles

Imagine that the part of you that wants to write is an adorable, excited, energetic little puppy. A puppy that is totally dependent upon you to keep him happy, well fed, and healthy. Here are some guidelines for caring for your writing puppy.

1. Love, honor, and respect your puppy.

2. Feed and walk your puppy every day.

3. Sometimes, let your puppy off the leash to run free.

4. Train your puppy to come when you call by using rewards and kind words, not intimidation.

5. Be firm and consistent with training, but don't break your puppy's spirit.

6. Housebreaking your puppy will be a gradual process: do not give the puppy a biscuit when he pees on the rug.

7. If you ignore your puppy all day, he might keep you awake at night or chew up your slippers.

8. Protect your puppy from harm.

9. Remember that your puppy likes to play with other puppies.

10. Play with your puppy, enjoy your puppy, love your puppy.

Bibliography

Benabou, Marcel. (1996). **Why I Have Not Written Any of My Books**. Lincoln: University of Nebraska Press.

Benchley, Robert. (2001). **The Benchley Roundup**. Chicago: University of Chicago Press.

Boice, Robert. (1994). **How Writers Journey to Comfort and Fluency**. Westport: Praeger. *A comprehensive description of his knowledge and advice for writers of all types.*

Boice, Robert. (1992a). "Combined treatments for writing blocks." **Behaviour Research and Therapy.** 30, 51–61.

Boice, Robert. (1990). **Professors as Writers**. Stillwater: New Forums. *A well-researched, balanced and practical guide focussed on improving productivity in academia, though it applies to all writers. Highly recommended.*

Bolker, Joan. (1997). **The Writer's Home Companion**. New York: Henry Holt.

Bolker, Joan. (1998). **Writing Your Dissertation in Fifteen Minutes a Day**. New York: Owl Books.

Boon, Marcus. (2002). **The Road of Excess**: **A History of Writers on Drugs**. Cambridge: Harvard University Press.

Burns, David. (1992). **Feeling Good**. New York: Avon. *Helpful techniques from cognitive therapy to address problems with perfectionism, negative self-talk, depression, anxiety, etc.*

Cameron, Julia. (1995). **The Artist's Way**. New York: Putnam. *The daily writing exercise prescribed in this book is potentially useful to all blocked writers.*

Bring Your Writing Back to Life!

Cameron, Julia. (1998). **The Right to Write**. New York: Tarcher/Putnam.

Charters, Ann. (1992). **The Portable Beat Reader**. New York: Penguin.

Dyer, Geoff. (1997). **Out of Sheer Rage**. New York: North Point Press. Dark, funny.

Elbow, Peter. (1973). **Writing Without Teachers**. New York: Oxford University Press. *Very good explanation and description of "freewriting."*

Evans-Wentz, W. Y. (ed.) (1960). **The Tibetan Book of the Dead**. London: Oxford University Press.

Faulkner, Raymond and Goelet, Ogden. (ed) (1998). **The Egyptian Book of the Dead: The Book of Going Forth by Day: Being the Papyrus of Ani**. San Francisco: Chronicle Books.

Flaherty, Alice, W. (2004). **The Midnight Disease**. New York: Houghton Mifflin. *A neurologist weighs in on writing and the brain.*

Goldberg, Natalie. (1990). **Wild Mind: Living the Writer's Life**. New York: Bantam.

Goldberg, Natalie. (1988). **Writing Down the Bones**. Boston: Shambala.

Harvey, Joan C. and Cynthia Katz. (1985). **If I'm So Successful, Why Do I Feel Like a Fake?** New York: St. Martin's.

Huddle, David. (1991). **The Writing Habit**: Essays. Salt Lake City: Gibbs-Smith.

Johnstone, Keith. (1992). **Impro: Improvisation and Theatre**. New York: Routledge. *An inspiring book on creativity and spontaneity.*

Kabot-Zinn, John. (2005). **Full Catastrophe Living**. New York: Bantam. *An introduction to mindfulness meditation as a way to relieve stress.*

Kellog, Ronald. (1994). **The Psychology of Writing**. New York: Oxford
University Press.

Kirsch, Gesa. (1993). **Women Writing the Academy**. Carbondale: Southern Illinois University Press. *Issues and challenges for women academic writers.*

Kornfeld, Jack. (1993). **A Path With Heart**. New York: Bantam. *A good explanation of the Buddhist approach to working with the mind.*

Lamott, Anne. (1994). **Bird by Bird**. New York: Pantheon. *This humane and very funny approach to the emotional challenges of being a writer is a morale booster.*

Miller, Henry. (1964). **Henry Miller on Writing**. New York: New Directions.

Moxley, J. and Lenker, L. (1995). **The Politics and Process of Scholarship**. Westport, CT: Greenwood Press. *Essays on a number of issues related to writing and publishing in academia.*

Olsen, Tillie. (1979). **Silences**. New York: Dell. *A women's account of the experience of being unable to write for years due to other responsibilities.*

Rico, Gabrielle. (1983). **Writing the Natural Way**. Los Angeles: Tarcher.

Rose, Mike. (1985). **When a Writer Can't Write**. New York: Guilford.

Steinbeck, John. (1989). **Working Days: The Journals of the Grapes of Wrath**. New York: Viking. *Even the greatest writers struggle.*

Sternberg, David. (1981). **How to Complete and Survive a Doctoral Dissertation**. New York: St. Martin's.

Valian, Virginia. (1977). "Learning to Work" in **Working it Out**. New York: Pantheon. *A great article on working with resistance.*

Weschler, Lawrence. (2000). "The Novelist and the Nun." *The New Yorker,* 10/2/2000, 74–86.

Zerubavel, Eviatar. (1999). **The Clockwork Muse**. Cambridge: Harvard University Press. *This book offers a systematic approach to organizing and writing big projects.*

About the Author

David A. Rasch, Ph.D.
Photo courtesy of Stanford University

David Rasch is a psychologist with 20 years of experience working with writers who struggle with blocks, procrastination, and other writing productivity problems. He has worked as a therapist, workshop leader, writing consultant, Director at Stanford University's Faculty Staff Help Center, and he currently serves as the Stanford University Ombuds. Dr. Rasch has given presentations about his work with faculty authors at state and national conferences and has spoken to numerous student and staff groups at Stanford and other universities nationwide. He has also offered talks and workshops attended by writers of poetry, fiction, journalism, academic research, nonfiction, business and technical writing, Web writing, and personal writing.

Dr. Rasch brings a compassionate, humorous, and insightful perspective to his work that combines his extensive psychological training and experience with practical advice for negotiating the daily challenges of the writing life. In addition to *The Blocked Writer's Book of the Dead,* his writing includes a chapter in the edited volume *Process and Organizational Redesign*, several magazine and newsletter articles, and more than a hundred songs. Dr. Rasch is President of the Central Coast Writers Branch of the California Writers Club and was recipient of their Centennial Short Story Award in 2009.

THE BLOCKED WRITER'S BOOK OF THE DEAD
WORKSHOP

David Rasch offers workshops and classes
for improving writing productivity,
and is available to speak to groups
interested in the topic.

David also consults individually with writers.

For more information, e-mail him at:
davidarnotrasch@gmail.com

CPSIA information can be obtained
at www.ICGtesting.com
Printed in the USA
FFHW011247110419
51690818-57111FF